The American
Legal Profession

To Diane

Sara Miller McCune founded SAGE Publishing in 1965 to support the dissemination of usable knowledge and educate a global community. SAGE publishes more than 1000 journals and over 800 new books each year, spanning a wide range of subject areas. Our growing selection of library products includes archives, data, case studies and video. SAGE remains majority owned by our founder and after her lifetime will become owned by a charitable trust that secures the company's continued independence.

Los Angeles | London | New Delhi | Singapore | Washington DC | Melbourne

The American Legal Profession

The Myths and Realities of Practicing Law

Christopher P. Banks

Kent State University

FOR INFORMATION:

CQ Press

An Imprint of SAGE Publications, Inc.

2455 Teller Road

Thousand Oaks, California 91320

E-mail: order@sagepub.com

SAGE Publications Ltd.

1 Oliver's Yard

55 City Road

London EC1Y 1SP

United Kingdom

SAGE Publications India Pvt. Ltd.

B 1/I 1 Mohan Cooperative Industrial Area

Mathura Road, New Delhi 110 044

India

SAGE Publications Asia-Pacific Pte. Ltd.

3 Church Street

#10-04 Samsung Hub

Singapore 049483

Copyright © 2018 by CQ Press, an Imprint of SAGE Publications, Inc. CQ Press is a registered trademark of Congressional Quarterly Inc.

All rights reserved. No part of this book may be reproduced or utilized in any form or by any means, electronic or mechanical, including photocopying, recording, or by any information storage and retrieval system, without permission in writing from the publisher.

Printed in the United States of America

Library of Congress Cataloging-in-Publication Data

Names: Banks, Christopher P., author.

Title: The American legal profession : the myths and realities of practicing law / Christopher P. Banks, Kent State University.

Description: Washington, DC : CQ Press, 2017. | Includes bibliographical references and index.

Identifiers: LCCN 2017007098 | ISBN 9781506333120 (pbk. : alk. paper)

Subjects: LCSH: Practice of law—United States. | Law—Vocational guidance—United States. | Lawyers—United States.

Classification: LCC KF300 .B35 2017 | DDC 340.023/73—dc23

LC record available at https://lccn.loc.gov/2017007098

This book is printed on acid-free paper.

Acquisitions Editors: Matthew Byrnie,
                        Monica Eckman

Editorial Assistant: Zachary Hoskins

Production Editor: Tracy Buyan

Copy Editor: Melinda Masson

Typesetter: C&M Digitals (P) Ltd.

Proofreader: Sally Scott

Indexer: Marilyn Augst

Cover Designer: Candice Harman

Marketing Manager: Jennifer Jones

SUSTAINABLE FORESTRY INITIATIVE   Certified Sourcing
www.sfiprogram.org
SFI-01075

17 18 19 20 21 10 9 8 7 6 5 4 3 2

Brief Contents

Detailed Contents

List of Tables and Figures

TABLES

FIGURES

Preface

Not too long ago, early in the spring semester, a student from my constitutional law civil rights and liberties course stopped by during office hours to discuss a grading issue. As we talked, I discovered that he was a senior majoring in political science; but I had never counseled him before, and it was the first time that I had seen him in any of my classes. I also learned that he had emigrated from a foreign country to complete his undergraduate degree at Kent State. Moreover, to my amazement, Civil Rights and Liberties, which is designed for upper-division undergraduate students, was his first "law" course. He was considering a prelaw minor, but was unsure. After we finished the business at hand, he then rather offhandedly mentioned to me that he had recently applied to law school with the intention of permanently staying in the United States to practice law as an attorney. At that point, I asked if he would be willing to tell me what his undergraduate grade-point average (UGPA) and Law School Admission Test (LSAT) scores were, and where he applied. He agreed to do so, and I learned he had sent applications to roughly nine schools across the country with a 3.2 UGPA and a 137 LSAT score. Depending on the cost of filing applications, I thought to myself that he probably had already spent hundreds of dollars in registration costs and fees in applying to a multitude of law schools.

With that information in hand, I gently told him that his chances of getting into law school were slim to nonexistent (at least relative to applications he submitted). He smiled at me and then expressed his confidence of getting in because he was retaking the LSAT in the *next two days*, offering that he would be assured admission if he raised his score to 145. He shared with me that prior to seeing me he did not get any prelaw advice from any university or department prelaw advisers, and that he did not take any LSAT preparation courses but rather adopted a self-help study strategy due to the high cost of the former. After I asked, he admitted that he did not spend the amount of time that I advise students to do in engaging in LSAT preparation (about two hundred hours or so of preparatory study). After absorbing these facts, I then pulled up the Law School Admission Council (LSAC) website (www.lsac.org) to show him what his probability of getting into law school was in light of his LSAT score and grade point average, among other things.

When I did so, *for the first time* he realized that his chance of admission was between 0 and 10 percent based on a statistical analysis of fall 2015 full-time application and admission data reported by law schools approved by the American Bar Association (ABA). With the LSAC site on my computer monitor in front of us, we learned that his chances improved somewhat in respect to only a handful of the two hundred or so ABA-approved law schools that exist nationwide; but he had never heard of those schools, so he did not target them as places to send applications (he also did not realize that they were less renowned ABA-approved schools; so, if he did get in, he was likely to incur high student loan debt and the risk of not paying his loans off easily because there were less realistic chances that he would secure profitable and stable employment after graduation).

While he was cognizant of the LSAC site (he had to be, in order to apply to law school), he was not aware of the "LSAC Resources" link at the top of the webpage; nor was he aware that if he highlighted it, he could access the "LSAC Official Guide to ABA-Approved Law Schools" (https://officialguide.lsac.org/release/OfficialGuide_Default.aspx), a resource that is used to learn whether law schools of interest are likely to admit, based on LSAT and UGPA results. I pulled out an old print version of the Official Guide from a bookshelf and briefly outlined the type of information and advice it gave to readers. The guide, as many prelaw advisers know, is a one-stop resource that conveys what the law school admission process is like, and it provides tips for understanding what skills lawyers have and what attorneys are likely to do in practice (notably, that information now digitally represents the content that was in the defunct print version, much to my "old school" disappointment).

Near the end of our chat, we talked about the implications of retaking the LSAT (what law schools might do if he did poorly again in light of his preexisting score) and how to study for it. I concluded the meeting by suggesting that he consult the Standard 509 Information Reports that law schools are now required to generate in light of the admissions scandals that have plagued them, especially in the aftermath of the 2008 recession. Although it remains a key consumer protection resource, the Standard 509 Information Reports are largely unknown to most applicants, even though they are discoverable on each law school's website, as well as from the ABA (http://abare quireddisclosures.org). Among other things, on an annual basis the reports provide data on the number of applications received by the law school, as well as how many applicants are admitted. It also gives summary statistics on tuition rates, grants and scholarships, class enrollment profiles, attrition and bar passage rates, and faculty and administrators; and, perhaps most important, it supplies a sense of whether applicants are likely to get in (or not) by providing a synopsis of admissions based on representative grade point averages and LSAT scores. After he looked at one of the reports, the student conceded that he wished he had known about them before he submitted his applications.

While I do not know what happened with my student, my guess is that he will struggle to get into law school; and, if he does get admitted, he might regret the choice to attend at all, when all is said and done (I hope not, though!). Sadly, the story I have just told is hardly unique and well known to most prelaw advisers at undergraduate universities and colleges across the country. The fact that it is a recurring scenario is one of the main reasons why I wrote this book. In my own experience, which extends to nearly a quarter-century of giving prelaw advice, I sur-mise that only a small fraction of the thousands of students I have advised have done the serious and time-consuming preparatory work that is required to apply to law school and also to learn what it is like to be in law school or to practice law. Like the student described above, my advisees typically have not carefully considered (1) the content or implications of their prelaw studies; (2) the actual cost, both in time and in money, to prepare for LSAT study, or to apply for and attend law school; and (3) the intricacies or logistics of graduate legal study, or what the implications are in securing a law degree and then moving into a sometimes unstable or unpredictable economy. They also do not know that law graduates have a variety of employment options beyond the practice of law. And they know very little, as well, about the multitude of issues and challenges that confront the legal profession, in terms of both theory and on-the-ground legal practice realities.

Most often, what most students interested in law as a career *think they know* about lawyering is derived from all-too-common and popular misconceptions about the American legal profession (which I call "myths" in the pages that follow). The myths are fueled by television shows, fictional books, advertisements, news and social media, anecdotes, and even sometimes the law schools themselves by way of their recruitment activities—everything but the facts and reality. A basic theme of the underlying myths is that they falsely imply to students that there is little cost, and only an upside, to being an attorney: most often, lawyers in shiny and expensive suits famously defend and argue their clients' cases in court after breezing through law school and then, with little difficulty, secure employment in well-paying law firms that generously supply them with all of the job security, and fancy perks and reputation, of being a legal professional. While some of that may certainly ring true for some law graduates, for many others the realities of law study and practice are quite different.

As a result, *The American Legal Profession: The Myths and Realities of Practicing Law* is written to dispel the common myths while familiarizing students and prelaw advisers with the practical realities of what is required to get into law school, and then to succeed in it and afterward, in either law or nonlegal employment. In this respect, the book is an unprecedented analysis of prelaw studies, law school instruction, and legal practice topics. While emphasizing that lawyers fulfill a vital but often misunderstood public function in society, it uses some of the common misconceptions, or myths, about the legal profession to demonstrate that the reality of being a lawyer is much different from what many undergraduate political science or law-related majors or minors believe it to be. As such, it is a brief primer or stand-alone textbook on what it is really like to go into the legal profession, from start to finish. Its goal is to give prelaw advisers, and law-related instructors, the tools to engage in extended discussions about what the American legal profession truly consists of, and represents, in the U.S. justice system.

By correcting the common misconceptions about the American legal profession, the book supplies undergraduates and others interested in law with the information they need to evaluate the legal profession and all that it offers not only as a viable career choice, but also in remaining the foundation for establishing sound, but sometimes controversial, legal and social policy. While accentuating the truth over myths, prelaw advisers and instructors can use the book to stress that lawyers play a vital role as agents of legal change. Simultaneously, they will not have to spend valuable office or class time to explain that modern legal instruction is limited by an adherence to legal doctrine at the expense of practical hands-on apprentice training; that lawyers are not always trained to be trial litigators or experts in oral arguments before rapt juries in courtrooms; that not all attorneys are guaranteed to have a lucrative career simply because they got into law school; that not all lawyers work in high-profile private law firms; that the legal profession is not that diverse in terms of gender, race, or educational backgrounds; and that the market for the delivery of legal services is rapidly evolving and breaking away from conventional norms and practices due to domestic and global competitive pressures.

By design and in line with its pedagogical purpose, *The American Legal Profession: The Myths and Realities of Practicing Law* is a succinct but balanced account of topics that are of great interest to students, prelaw advisers, and scholars alike. It does not take sides or spend most of its time criticizing the state of the legal academy or the profession as a whole; yet it does not shrink from exposing some of the most common critiques. Its objective is to take what I call a "tough love" approach to the subject matter, with the expectation that those who read it will acquire the type of information that will greatly assist in the pursuit of a long, stable, and happy life in the law or in employment that can best lead to professional success, in or out of actual law practice. The book's goal is not to discourage those interested in pursuing law from following their dreams; rather, it is simply to educate and to give would-be attorneys the best chance to find a fruitful path in the law by informing them of the pros and cons of entering into the legal profession.

Chapter 1 introduces readers to three of the most popular myths and realities underlying the legal profession—the trial lawyer, "law school is a good investment," and diversity and egalitarian myths. These topics establish the foundation for the ensuing chapters. After introducing readers to lawyer demographics, legal practice settings, lawyer salaries, and the key issue of student loan debt, **Chapter 2** is a nuts-and-bolts description of how to prepare for, and apply to, law school. It analyzes the nature of prelaw undergraduate study, the importance of the LSAT, and how to evaluate rankings and other factors in selecting the "right" law school. It also explains the logistics of preparing law school applications. **Chapter 3** is a brief journey about what students can expect once they matriculate into law school. It explores the strengths and weaknesses of the so-called casebook method of legal training and the significance of the law school curriculum; it also gives instruction on what is required for bar admission. In addressing the practice of law, **Chapter 4** instructs students about what type of employment they can expect to secure once they graduate and enter the labor market. Specifically, it analyzes the business of legal practice, the impact that Big Law (corporate law practice in large elite law firms) has on the legal profession, the difference between private practice and other legal employment settings, and, perhaps most important (these days), the increasing prevalence of pursuing alternative nonlegal careers, or nonlegal jobs that take advantage of law-based training. The last chapter, **Chapter 5**, confronts the challenges facing the American legal profession in light of persistent criticisms that it needs reform. It surveys a variety of reform issues, including the implications of the legal profession's insularity in regulating certain facets of legal education, legal practice conditions, multijurisdictional and multidisciplinary practice, nonlawyer investment, and lawyer discipline. It then evaluates the viability of traditional law school instruction in light of the claim that it is a flawed pedagogy that does not prepare students for legal practice or give them the basis to learn professional identity skills or find decent employment; and it also analyzes whether technological changes and global competitive pressures that provide a low-cost method of solving legal problems will force changes in the way law is practiced in the legal services marketplace.

ACKNOWLEDGMENTS

Writing this book is something that I was probably destined to do in light of my current academic interests and my earlier professional experience as a lawyer, teacher, and occasional political candidate for public office. Still, as with any research project, I had much help in putting it together. Foremost, the undergraduate and graduate students I taught at the University of Virginia, the University of Akron, Kent State University, and elsewhere are responsible for giving me the insight about the nuances of prelaw study, the law school application process, and legal practice. Several faculty colleagues and graduate students have contributed to the research and writing process. In particular, Travis Watson, a recent law graduate and doctoral student in Kent State University's political science program, took the time to research some of the basic issues and offer a contemporary sounding board for my thoughts. The textbook could not have been written without the enthusiastic support from Sarah Calabi, who worked with me as an acquisitions editor from SAGE/CQ Press for my coauthored *The Judicial Process: Law, Courts, and Judicial Politics* (SAGE/CQ Press, 2015) (with David M. O'Brien). Associate director and interim editor Matthew Byrnie's timely intervention and support were also very instrumental in bringing the book to publication, along with his assistant, Zachary Hoskins. During the production process, the expertise and assistance from Tracy Buyan, Melinda Masson, Candice Harman, and Jennifer Jones, among others, were essential to getting the textbook published and marketed successfully. I would also like to thank the following reviewers for their valuable insight and suggestions:

Eric Bellone (Suffolk University)

Sandra Browning (University of Cincinnati)

Laura Fidelie (Midwestern State University)

Charles Jacobs (St. Norbert College)

Douglas Klutz (University of Alabama)

Donald A. Nielsen (College of Charleston)

Colin Wark (Texas A&M University–Kingsville)

Last but certainly not least, I want to acknowledge my family, especially my son, Zachary, and my daughter, Samantha, for having the patience to put up with me during the writing process; and, of course, my wife, Diane, who has put up with me with regard to everything for over twenty-five years. I dedicate this book to her, as she is undeniably the yin to my yang.

About the Author

Christopher P. Banks is a professor of political science at Kent State University. In 1980, he earned his BA in political science, and in 1984, he graduated with his law degree from the University of Dayton School of Law. Before receiving his doctorate in American politics from the University of Virginia in 1995, he practiced law in civil and criminal litigation in Connecticut and was active in local and state politics. He ran for state representative in 1988; after the election, he was appointed by Governor William O'Neill to serve as an administrative hearing officer for the Connecticut Commission on Human Rights and Opportunities. After graduating from the University of Virginia, he taught at the University of Akron for eleven years in the political science department. At Kent State University, he has served as the Department of Political Science's graduate coordinator for its MA and PhD programs, as well as an affiliate for the Center for Public Administration and Public Policy (now called the Center for Public Policy and Health). He has served as the prelaw adviser at Kent State and the University of Akron. At Kent State, he regularly teaches undergraduate and graduate courses in the judicial process, constitutional law, government powers, civil rights and liberties, law and society, criminal justice, terrorism, American political theory, and American politics. He is the author of *Judicial Politics in the D.C. Circuit Court* (John Hopkins University Press, 1999); coauthor of *The Judicial Process: Law, Courts, and Judicial Politics* (SAGE/CQ Press, 2015), *The U.S. Supreme Court and New Federalism: From the Rehnquist to the Roberts Court* (Rowman & Littlefield, 2012), and *Courts and Judicial Policymaking* (Prentice Hall, 2008); editor and chapter contributor of *The State and Federal Courts: A Complete Guide to History, Powers, and Controversy* (ABC-CLIO, 2017); and coeditor and chapter contributor of *The Final Arbiter: The Consequences of* Bush v. Gore *for Law and Politics* (State University of New York Press, 2006) and *Superintending Democracy: The Courts and the Political Process* (University of Akron Press, 2001). His numerous book chapters, book reviews, and journal articles on U.S. Supreme Court politics, judicial behavior, law and politics, federalism, terrorism, and human rights have appeared in *PS: Political Science & Politics, Justice System Journal, Publius: The Journal of Federalism, Judicature, Terrorism and Political Violence, International Journal of Human Rights, Public Integrity: A Journal of the American Society for Public Administration, Social Science Quarterly, Southeastern Political Review* (currently titled *Politics & Policy*), and *Journal of Law & Politics*, among others.

1 The Myths and Realities of Being a Lawyer

Many students interested in the legal profession simply do not know what lawyers do or what they represent to American society. Regardless of how they are perceived, it is difficult to dispute that lawyers can be a positive good for society because they are public servants who make enduring contributions to the law's development and they advance community and client interests. One practitioner with fifty years of experience explained that his first attraction and ultimate love affair with the law was grounded in his respect for "the crucial role lawyers have played in creating and shaping our nation" because attorneys "had unique abilities to help those in crisis and to ensure that equal justice and fairness were more than abstract principles." With their specialized understanding of the law and its impact, lawyers remain at the forefront of making important legal and political changes to American society. As examples, the practitioner praised "the lawyers who spearheaded the landmark case of *Brown v. Board of Education* (1954)," which broke down racial barriers by integrating public schools. He also admired "the exploits of Clarence Darrow, [a] courageous defender of unpopular persons and causes." Darrow was a special inspiration because he represented a high school science teacher who was prosecuted for teaching evolution in the famous Scopes Monkey Trial, among others. For this practitioner and surely for others like him, lawyers like these are simply the unsung heroes of American society.[1]

Envisioning lawyers as virtuous and impartial advocates of truth and justice is infused into American popular culture. Especially since the mid 1950s, the stories that surround fictional and nonfictional lawyer heroes like Atticus Finch (from the book and film *To Kill a Mockingbird*), Perry Mason (from the TV show *Perry Mason*), and F. Lee Bailey (a famous trial lawyer) reinforce the impression that attorneys selflessly represent idealistic notions of equality, fairness, and justice.[2] While scholars observe that lawyers were never very popular figures in early English or American history,[3] in the 1830s the French philosopher Alexis de Tocqueville countered that lawyers, judges, and the legal profession in general were critical to sustaining the political values underlying democratic governance and individual liberties. Fearful of the negative implications of popular majority rule, Tocqueville reasoned that an active, and educated, elite lawyer class was a crucial counterweight to the ill effects of unrestrained democratic rule and repressive public opinion. In particular, lawyers prevented ordinary citizens from becoming too detached from communal life, which ran the risk of allowing government to step into civil affairs more aggressively and therefore threaten personal freedoms. In his famous *Democracy in America* exposition, Tocqueville concluded that judges were virtuous political statesmen and that lawyers, as a class, are uniquely equipped to perform public service because of their specialized knowledge of the law.[4]

In spite of Tocqueville's teachings, many critics today are quick to point out that the legal profession is in crisis.[5] Public opinion polls are cited to show that not too many citizens believe that lawyers contribute much to society.[6] Underlying the poll results are a litany of common complaints made by legal scholars and practitioners in the field: (1) law school tuition is skyrocketing, and law school costs too much to attend; (2) many students struggle to find a job and pay down hundreds of thousands of dollars of unsustainable student loan debt after they graduate; (3) law school education is flawed because it does not adequately teach clinical skills, and it is poor preparation for students seeking to compete in an increasingly globalized and technologically sophisticated work space; (4) the legal profession is homogeneous, elitist, and stratified into the haves and the have-nots, with little diversity; (5) most private law practice, especially in what is pejoratively known as Big Law, is driven by profit, and it has become more of a business and less of a profession; and (6) as an educational investment, a law degree is simply not worth it.[7] Law professor Deborah L. Rhode thus flatly declares that the legal profession is in steep decline in many critical areas of legal education, law practice, and professional regulation.[8]

This book explores some of these criticisms in an effort to separate fact from fiction and to dispel some of the common misconceptions surrounding the American legal profession. It does so by offering a condensed version of the nuts and bolts of the American legal profession. After discussing some of the common myths surrounding lawyers and legal practice, it supplies key information about the prelaw admission process. Thereafter, it turns to explaining the challenges that law school students face not only in law school but also after they pass the bar and endeavor to secure employment in the attempt to practice law. A final consideration is to analyze where the legal profession is headed in the twenty-first century, amid the oft repeated clarion call for reform. A full understanding of what the realities are in the legal profession, though, requires deconstructing some of the most prevalent misconceptions about lawyers and the legal profession.

THE TRIAL LAWYER MYTH

Popular renditions of lawyers portray them as always discovering the truth and achieving justice through courtroom trials in perpetually interesting and controversial cases.[9] In part, the perception flows from the folksy homespun image of a lawyer's professional identity. The homespun image is inspired by Harper Lee's portrayal of model country lawyer Atticus Finch in her famous *To Kill a Mockingbird* (1962). This archetype, which commands respect and community veneration, depicts lawyers as consummate professionals who are selfless, civic minded, and fierce advocates not only of the rule of law but also of clients' interests. Undeterred by popular passions and causes, Atticus Finch–type lawyers exercise the independent judgment that makes them specially qualified to perform their lawyer role with dignity and honor, a trait that makes them an attractive resource to handle difficult problems or cases in times of legal trouble.[10]

Especially in older films, lawyers are similarly portrayed as the main protagonist in courtroom dramas that register their willingness to come to the "defense of the downtrodden," which is also part of their unwavering commitment to "battling for civil liberties, or single-handedly preventing injustice."[11] This image of the gallant public servant, which some scholars link to the proprietary advocacy interests of the American Bar Association,[12] is reinforced by traditional media and real-life examples. In the film version of *To Kill a Mockingbird*, country lawyer Atticus Finch zealously defends and protects the dignity of a poor black man who is wrongly accused of raping a young white woman in a southern Alabama town during the Depression. After he saves his client from a lynch mob and displays his remarkable talents as a trial lawyer in a packed courtroom, an all-white jury disregards the evidence that Finch has skillfully presented and convicts the black defendant, who is later killed when he tries to escape. As the story unfolds, Finch shows another side to his character after he chooses to cover up the truth about who killed the young white woman's father, who was trying to harm Finch's children after the trial. As a result, in taking on the case, Finch takes many professional risks that place him and his family in mortal danger; and, in covering up the truth about who killed the white girl's father, Finch shows another side of his humanity by making a complex moral judgment that it is better to protect the real killer, or "mockingbird" (Boo Radley), whose life would be destroyed if he were criminally prosecuted in trying to help protect Finch's children.[13]

At times, the Atticus Finch portrayal of lawyers and the legal system is illustrated and reinforced by parallel real-life dramas. In *Powell v. Alabama* (1932), the Supreme Court ruled that the Constitution and its principle of having a fair trial require that defendants must have counsel appointed for them in cases involving the imposition of capital punishment. Roughly thirty years later, in *Gideon v. Wainwright* (1963), the Supreme Court built upon the *Powell* precedent by expanding the Sixth Amendment right to have appointed counsel for indigent defendants who need it in all state capital and noncapital prosecutions. In addition, today there are many "unsung heroes in law offices everywhere working competently for ordinary modest fees," as well as "numerous lawyers serving *pro bono* in public interest cases or volunteering in clinics" or otherwise engaged in modest-paying government jobs in order to enforce environmental protection laws or worker safety.[14] Still, while much of this under-the-radar work may go unnoticed or even unappreciated by the public, the popular conception that many lawyers live their professional lives in courtroom dramas by arguing cases as trial counsel is an oversimplification of reality.

The Reality

The country lawyer archetype is a distortion of reality because it portrays the lawyering "as we wish it really was and as it sometimes, though rarely, really is."[15] Although the popular images of what lawyers do are shaped through a variety of media formats (e.g., prime-time television, movies, news outlets, best-selling books, and stand-up comedy or lawyer jokes), clearly the images that are being sent are exaggerated and oftentimes misleading.[16] While the public image of the law and legal profession was quite positive during what some describe as the golden age of the legal profession in film in the 1960s,[17] both historical and contemporary descriptions of attorneys consistently characterize them as pejorative "banditti, as blood-suckers, as pick-pockets, as wind-bags, as smooth-tongued rogues"[18]; or as "money-hungry," "boozed-out," "burned-out," "incompetent," "unethical sleazebags" who are deceitful tricksters, or shysters.[19] In fact, lawyers have never been popular as a group. In colonial times, the perception that attorneys were predators led to denouncements that they were "cursed Hungry Caterpillars [who charge] fees that eat out the very bowels of [the] Commonwealth." In many ways, that depiction of the attorney role still resonates today with misplaced criticisms that lawyers are predominantly arrogant, greedy, and egotistical single-minded seekers of lawsuit profits, a portrayal captured in films like *The Devil's Advocate* (with Keanu Reeves and Al Pacino, the latter of whom plays Satan) and *The Verdict* (with Paul Newman depicting an alcoholic and ethically challenged ambulance chaser pitted against a slick and duplicitous opponent from a big law firm), among others.[20]

While many citizens are satisfied and respect the performance of their own respective lawyers, when the public evaluates the legal profession as a whole, a more negative picture emerges.[21] Lawyers thus become easy targets and scapegoats for blame because it is difficult to disassociate them from the dim view the public has about the nature and operation of the adversary legal system.[22] From the public's perspective, lawyers are often criticized for being greedy, dishonest, uncivil, arrogant, and neglectful of client needs. This assessment puts lawyers in a bad light because they overcharge for services that could be done by laymen; they use their legal knowledge to free unpopular clients who ought to be held criminally responsible for their actions; they financially or professionally capitalize on representing clients facing the worst sort of legal difficulties, including personal injuries, bankruptcies, divorce, or contract disputes; or they contribute to the problems of delay and expense that are commonly associated with an overburdened adversary litigation process that can only deliver legal services to the rich.[23] The notion that there are too many lawyers and that they overlitigate to harm the nation's economy is reported by public opinion polls and conservative interest groups or politicians that blame trial lawyers for abusing the tort system by filing frivolous and class action lawsuits, among other things.[24] For these reasons and others, "It's almost impossible to go too far when it comes to demonizing lawyers," in part because many of the "perceived abuses [are being committed] by other people's lawyers and a system that fails to correct those abuses."[25]

Beyond their public image, the myth that attorneys primarily engage in trial work ignores the fact that most lawyers rarely step inside a courtroom and, if they do, almost all of the cases are settled well before a jury has the chance to deliberate on a verdict. The common public perceptions surrounding trial work and all it entails are simply inaccurate on a variety of levels.[26] While a majority of lawyers are engaged in private practice, there is little empirical evidence to show that lawyers overlitigate or abuse their responsibilities in resolving disputes.[27] In fact, studies have indicated that there are many psychological, financial, and time management disincentives for litigants to sue, and that most of the grievances by citizens have rarely become full-blown legal disputes that require formal action by lawyers or the legal system.[28]

In addition, if an attorney does step inside a courtroom to try a case, workload statistics and academic studies demonstrate that presenting a case to a jury at the last stage of the judicial process is more the exception than the rule because 95 percent or more of civil and criminal cases are resolved by a negotiated settlement or plea bargain.[29] As a result, today many scholars depict the judicial process as an era of the "vanishing trial," and one that very rarely gives attorneys the opportunity to showcase their talents before a jury or a judge through a compelling oral argument.[30] Indeed, lawyers generally today must advance their arguments by written briefs that courts respond to by issuing summary dispositions or dismissals that forego the need for a trial. As one example, on the federal appellate level, the percentage of appeals that are terminated on their merits after an oral hearing has sharply declined over time from the mid-1980s to 2013, dropping from 56 to 18 percent of appeals.[31] The disappearance of oral arguments and trials from the legal landscape, when combined with the increasing use of alternative dispute systems like arbitration, mediation, and the like, affords little opportunity for Atticus Finch archetype lawyers, or any other kind of attorney, to make their case in court or before a jury.[32]

THE "LAW SCHOOL IS A GOOD INVESTMENT" MYTH

Census and labor statistics, plus survey data from the Pew Research Center, reinforce the positive effect that earning a professional degree has on lifetime earnings. A 2002 Census Bureau report found that persons with an advanced professional degree (in the medical or legal field) earned a yearly average of $99,300 whereas college graduates ($45,400), high school graduates ($25,900), and high school dropouts ($18,900) earned far less. Over the span of forty years, professional degree holders could thus expect to earn twice as much ($4.4 million) as individuals who only went to college for four years ($2.1 million). A 2013 report, published by a law professor and a finance and economics professor, estimated that law graduates would earn $1 million more in a lifetime than others who only had a bachelor's degree.[33] The 2011 Pew assessment had similar findings, but went further in concluding that the added value of a law degree over a forty-year work life ($1.2 million) would most likely exceed the cost of earning it (then estimated at $75,000 for going to law school, plus $96,000 in lost earnings).[34] Moreover, for 2015, a Bureau of Labor Statistics employment projection stated that lawyers could expect to make a median average salary of $115,820.[35]

In light of these numbers and forecasts, it is reasonable to think that students are attracted to the law because they envision the legal profession as a stable career choice that increases the chances for achieving lifelong job security, a respectable income, and status, power, or prestige within a community. However, students with this impression often see the legal profession through the lens of popular culture, which distorts what the law is or what lawyers represent.[36] In essence, students of this mindset apply to law school since there is a "broad cultural mythology about lawyers—simultaneously loathed, admired, envied, and feared—[which] runs through American society, built up in history, fiction, and popular television and movies."[37]

With television shows like *L.A. Law* and *Boston Legal* or best-selling books such as John Grisham's *The Firm*, it is easy for students to conclude that lawyers are rich, good-looking, and smart individuals who work in top-tier affluent law firms. These students may read newspaper stories or collect anecdotal information that suggests that corporate lawyers (those who work in what is often called Big Law) make six-figure incomes directly after graduating from law school.[38] As one scholar explains:

> Tens of thousands of people apply to law school each year because it is an avenue to a desirable career. There is prestige attached to the status of

a lawyer. Lawyers are smart professionals who wear suits. Most lawyers earn a comfortable living, and very successful ones become wealthy. Many lawyers play leading roles in advising or managing corporations. Many public figures are lawyers. One can do good things as a lawyer—support a cause, work in public service, prosecute criminals, become a politician, serve as a judge, become a high-level government official, advocate for the poor, defend the unjustly accused. Lawyers are pillars of the community.[39]

This portrayal of lawyering turns the legal profession into a largely win-win career strategy, with little risk and a great upside. In this regard, pursuing a law degree is an optimal career choice because it can be functionally applied to a variety of business, government, and other community settings that expand the range of employment possibilities in new and exciting ways. In short, "it is a good bet for a prestigious, lucrative career."[40]

The Reality

Students held under the sway of the American legal profession mystique are hampered in making a sound career choice because they are ignorant of what lawyers do or how much they make in a professional career.[41] To the extent it exists, the societal perception that lawyers are high-status professionals who do socially meaningful work for large sums of money is deeply flawed.[42] At least part of the misconception is explained by the type of student who is drawn to law school in the first place. Students entering into legal study share a number of "lawyer attributes," or preexisting personality traits, that are developed in their childhood, including dominance and leadership, self-discipline, school achievement, and an affinity toward reading. Also, prelaw students have a higher-than-average socioeconomic status and tend to be proactive in their environments. Many share an aversion toward math or the hard sciences, or being subordinate or deferential. Moreover, prelaw students go into law because it provides intellectual stimulation and the best chance to earn materialistic gains or prestige. While other drivers of prelaw interest are rooted in altruism or a desire to give back to the community, scholars argue that some prelaw students perceive law school as a "residual graduate school," or default career option that remains attractive for applicants who are uncertain about, or uncommitted to, their career path.[43] As one analyst quipped, law school is "the traditional default option for students with no idea what to do with their lives."[44] This motivation is especially prevalent among the well-to-do, who choose law because it does not require any specialized training or, quite simply, they could not get into medical school or do anything else that was considered professionally respectable.[45]

Other scholarship postulates there are two groups of students who vie for law school admission. Among the first group are those who express a commitment to pursing a legal career early on. In one survey, roughly a third of law school applicants stated that they knew since childhood that they intended to go to law school after college.[46] For these students, either an interest in law was created by the experience of a defining accomplishment (like finding success in a high school mock trial exercise or a high school debate), or they grew up in a household with professionally employed parents who impressed upon them the benefits of earning a law degree. In college, these students elect a major concentration in one of the social sciences, such as political science, prelaw, or history; but, significantly, they do so without seriously thinking about an alternative career path.[47]

In contrast, another group of applicants, who represent about a third of survey respondents, make their decision to go to law school while they are undergraduates.[48] These types of applicants are susceptible to the popular imagery of media-generated attorneys or otherwise are motivated by the prospect of making money.[49] While they have a vague interest in law, either personal circumstances or prevailing marketplace conditions compel them to apply.[50] Students in this mind-set share the conventional view that law school is a "safe harbor for a poor economy," a belief that is supported by the fact that application rates tend to rise and fall in accordance with market conditions.[51] Students within this category, then, might be recent college graduates who get laid off from their jobs or who wish to escape a low-paying job or dissatisfying employment. Accordingly, a legal career is desirable because "it is perceived to be a good way to wait out a recession and retool to enter the job market with a new set of opportunities."[52]

Understanding the motivations for going to law school is important because students from either group may harbor the false impression that becoming a lawyer is a surefire ticket to earning professional success and a respectable standard of living. Although some students acknowledge the risk that their law career may not pan out, many others simply assume that whatever costs they expend in applying to and attending law school will eventually be absorbed or recouped over the long haul by the considerable amount of lifetime earnings they will make as a successful lawyer. Notably, this presumption is reinforced by law school deans and recruiters who maintain that obtaining a law degree is a wise educational investment that reaps significant long-term material and intangible benefits over the lifetime of a professional career.[53]

Still, making the presumption that earning a law degree is an absolute guaranty of job security and lucrative professional success is precarious at best. Although the issue of whether law school is "worth it" as a lifetime investment remains an elusive question to answer definitively, clearly a host of personal and economic factors that are unique to the applicant ultimately shape the success or failure of a professional career path.[54] While many law graduates do indeed find professional success and satisfaction, empirical research demonstrates that for many others "law school is a very risky (and expensive) investment; [and that] it should not be entered into lightly."[55] A number of factors, including the high cost of law school tuition, rising student loan debt, and the uncertainty of finding a job after graduating from law school, weigh heavily in the calculus of whether making an investment in the law is worth it.

THE DIVERSITY AND EGALITARIAN MYTH

The United States was founded on ideals of law and justice that are central to not only its constitutional heritage but also its cultural identity as a representative republic. Key democratic values, such as political representation, self-government by popular rule, and the separation of powers among legislative, executive, and judicial institutions, define the unique relationship that government has to individual rights in society. Among the most treasured and valued principles of this heritage of political freedom is "equal justice under the law," an ideal that "embellishes courthouse entrances, ceremonial occasions, and constitutional decisions" because it is "central to the legitimacy of democratic processes."[56] Equally compelling are corresponding beliefs, norms, and expectations that all legal institutions, including lawyers, judges, and the organized bar, represent those ideals. As one legal scholar put it, the pillars at the base of the Declaration of Independence, namely equality, natural "unalienable" rights, and the consent of the governed, are fabled and ingrained truths of "all professional utterances of lawyers."[57]

It is logical to assume that because equality is a cornerstone of American governance it should extend in practice to having an equal opportunity to become part of the legal profession and the fight for justice. Indeed, this was the case early on in U.S. history even though lawyers were never particularly well liked. In the aftermath of the American Revolution, the lawyer class proliferated, in large part because the legal profession as we know it today did not exist: there were no law schools or organized bar, and the regulations governing legal practice were scant. As one legal scholar notes, by the mid-nineteenth century "every state loosened their entry requirements, and many states allowed any citizen to appear in court or practice law."[58] Moreover, culturally law was seen as a path to social advancement and upward mobility that was, in theory, open to all. Pursuing a law degree, therefore, was part of the American Dream and "a ladder to success, financially and politically." While race, class, and family background (and being a male) mattered, in theory "everyone had a fighting chance to succeed" in law. With few regulatory or law licensing constraints in place, formal entry into what loosely could be called an organized legal profession was relatively easy and virtually unrestricted up until the turn of the twentieth century.[59]

The Reality

Today, the legal profession consists of practicing lawyers, the organized bar, the judiciary, and the legal academy. Each facet of the profession has evolved from elitist and homogeneous roots that have only slowly become more diversified by class, gender, and race over time. Early in U.S. history, bar admission standards were lax until they were tightened up by lawyer elites who began to organize into local, state, and national bar associations that were interested in keeping lawyers out of the profession instead of letting them in. The American Bar Association, formed in 1878, purported to represent all lawyers; but, in reality, it expressed the interests of a narrow set of corporate lawyers who were primarily beholden to the influence of railroads, utilities, and business interests. For the first fifty years of its existence, all of the ABA presidents and its committee membership were men and white, and most were affluent and Protestant. Indeed, for much of this time period, the organized bar directed its political efforts at retaining the influence of white Anglo-Saxon corporate lawyer elites who were increasingly threatened by an influx of immigrants that came to America during industrialization.[60]

By the twentieth century, the corporate bar worked with the ABA, the Association of American Law Schools, and state and local bar associations to restrict the entry of immigrants into the profession. Industrial and urban immigrants, who were perceived as an "underclass" that threatened the bar's "purity," were a competitive threat to the established elite because they used contingency fees and new advertising practices in cities to create lawsuits for the working class that undermined corporate interests and profits. As one scholar puts it, the bar thus used its influence to "keep the immigrants out of the profession, exert control over those already in, and cripple the practice and effectiveness of those who could not be kept out or thrown out."[61]

The organized bar adopted several regulatory strategies to accomplish these goals. Law schools seeking ABA accreditation had to employ full-time faculty and require a college education for admission; law schools conditioned admission on English-speaking literacy skills or sponsorship from a practicing member of the bar; approvals of part-time night or commercial schools were increasingly denied; bar admission was restricted to those with citizenship and having "good" character; integrated (mandatory) bar requirements forced immigrant lawyers to join a bar association in the state they practiced in; and new ethical codes were devised to restrict ambulance-chasing activities, undesirable advertising practices, and the use of contingency fees.[62] During this formative period of the nascent legal profession, the elite's desire to maintain the status quo exposed the myth that anyone could be a lawyer. As one critic explains:

> According to idyllic folklore, the doors of access to the legal profession always swung open to anyone stung by ambition; lawyers might prefer a restricted guild, but democratic realities required them to settle for less. But this is a half-truth, which conceals the fact that the doors to particular legal careers required keys that were distributed according to race, religion, sex, and ethnicity. In fact, what the profession settled for was much less than the folklore promised.[63]

Notably, the difficulties nonelites had in gaining entry into the profession were also manifested by the stratification of the corporate bar in the early twentieth century: in urban areas, one segment of corporate lawyers were the elites, whereas nonprivileged ethnic lawyers were designated to represent the underclass.[64] Splitting the bar into the haves and the have-nots of the profession in this fashion is a forerunner to what scholars today refer to as the two hemispheres of legal practice, where lawyer elites from the best law schools represent large corporate interests that are affluent and everybody else delivers legal services to smaller businesses, governments, and individuals who are less endowed.[65]

Clearly, immigrants as well as women and people of color or different ethnicities have begun to integrate their ranks into the legal profession over the past half-century. But change has been slow in coming. To illustrate, the demographic characteristics of the state and federal courts register a professionalized (or "career") judiciary composed of judges who are predominantly white, male, Protestant, and affluent.[66] Until the 1960s and 1970s, women constituted roughly 3 percent of lawyers who, before then, were largely relegated to practice law in less prestigious practice settings and specialty areas. Persons of color as well as ethnic minorities faced even greater constraints in trying to enter into and succeed in the legal profession. While women now represent about a third of the legal profession (and minorities about a fifth), a variety of entrenched biases, stereotypes, and workplace structures still present the type of unique, significant, and ongoing challenges for the affected groups in their attempts to advance their careers and ultimately find professional satisfaction after graduating from law school.[67] Moreover, while one empirical study concludes that the legal profession is as diverse as other similarly prestigious (e.g., medical or dental) professions, it also finds that African Americans and Hispanic Americans are "*woefully* underrepresented in the legal profession when compared to their ratios in the U.S. population." As well, Asian Americans are identically poorly represented in the American legal profession.[68]

THE PLAN OF THE BOOK

The myths and realities just discussed are only three among a host of others that pervade the American legal profession. While the contrast between fact and fiction is often stark, an analysis of their differences should never mask the optimistic reality that many law students wind up with satisfying careers even in challenging times. After giving a brief overview of the legal profession, the next chapter addresses some of the common misconceptions about the nature of prelaw study and the process of applying to law school. For example, students interested in pursuing legal careers often believe that declaring certain majors, such as political science, is the only and perhaps best preparation for law study; or that the Law School Admission Test (LSAT), a prerequisite for applying to law school, is an examination that tests a person's knowledge of the law. While political science majors do often apply to law school, the reality is that there is no "prelaw" course of study that best prepares students for the rigors of getting a law degree, and the LSAT is not a test that examines whether a person knows the law. In addition, Chapter 2 exposes the risk of relying too much on the *U.S. News & World Report's* law school rankings in making application decisions and, instead, offers some guidance in preparing law school applications and determining where to send them.

In Chapter 3, some of the myths associated with legal education are discussed, including the conventional wisdom that law school actually trains lawyers to practice law. As the chapter explains, serving as an apprentice in a law office under the supervision of a licensed practitioner has largely been replaced by law school instruction through the casebook method, which teaches law students about legal doctrine in a case-dialogue, Socratic method. Some other popular beliefs—such as the preconceptions that law schools mostly offer "practice-ready" courses or that law instruction and grading is accomplished in the same type of format that students are used to in earning their undergraduate degrees—are also debunked. Additional misconceptions relating to licensing requirements and bar admissions are also analyzed and juxtaposed against the practice of law realities.

In Chapter 4, the practice of law is discussed in light of the conventional view that the law is a profession, not a business. While lawyers are most certainly licensed professionals, many reformers and critics of the legal profession argue that some of its core values, such as providing access to courts and legal services to those who need it the most, are compromised by an overarching need to make money. In this context, the business of legal practice is analyzed in terms of the legal profession's elitism, the growth of Big Law, and the various options lawyers have in selecting careers in different practice (and nonlegal) employment settings.

The book's concluding chapter addresses some of the major trends and reform issues that challenge the structure and integrity of the American legal profession. For numerous scholars, many of the issues, myths, and realities that are raised in the earlier chapters—among them, elitism, lack of diversity, high tuition rates, student loan debt, declining law school enrollments, inadequate legal instruction, and the difficulty of finding employment in a competitive job market—signal that the legal profession is in a state of crisis and must be reformed. Three areas of reform are discussed: (1) the legal profession's insularity and its resistance to effectuating reforming legal education and the conditions of practice, (2) the difficulties and challenges of reforming traditional legal instruction, and (3) whether the legal profession can continue to deliver legal services in a hypercompetitive and globalized marketplace in light of rapidly evolving technological changes and ongoing economic realities. These systemic issues are significant because it remains an open question as to whether the legal profession can continue to remain faithful to its professional values and ideals without taking remedial steps to reform some of its traditional regulatory structures, norms, and practices.

SELECTED READINGS

Asimow, Michael. "When Lawyers Were Heroes." *University of San Francisco Law Review* 30 (1996): 1131–1138.

Banks, Christopher P., and David M. O'Brien. *The Judicial Process: Law, Courts, and Judicial Politics.* Thousand Oaks, Calif.: Sage/CQ Press, 2015.

Chase, Anthony. "Lawyers and Popular Culture: A Review of Mass Media Portrayals of American Attorneys." *American Bar Foundation Research Journal* 11 (1986): 281–300.

Felstiner, William L. F., Richard L. Abel, and Austin Sarat. "The Emergence and Transformation of Disputes: Naming, Blaming, and Claiming." *Law and Society Review* 15 (1980–1981): 631–654.

Galanter, Marc. "The Vanishing Trial: An Examination of Trials and Related Matters in Federal and State Courts." *Journal of Empirical Legal Studies* 1 (1983): 459–570.

Harper, Steven J. *The Lawyer Bubble: A Profession in Crisis.* New York, N.Y.: Basic Books, 2013.

Krantz, Sheldon. *The Legal Profession: What Is Wrong and How to Fix It.* New Providence, N.J.: LexisNexis, 2014.

Mindes, Marvin W., and Alan C. Acock. "Trickster, Hero, Helper: A Report on the Lawyer Image." *American Bar Foundation Research Journal* 7 (1982): 177–233.

Moliterno, James E. *The American Legal Profession in Crisis: Resistance and Responses to Change.* New York, N.Y.: Oxford University Press, 2010.

Morgan, Thomas D. *The Vanishing Lawyer.* New York, N.Y.: Oxford University Press, 2010.

Rhode, Deborah L. *The Trouble with Lawyers.* New York, N.Y.: Oxford University Press, 2015.

WEB LINKS

Above the Law (http://abovethelaw.com)
American Bar Association (www.americanbar.org/aba.html)
Jurist (www.jurist.org)
Law Professor Blogs Network (www.lawprofessorblogs.com)

ENDNOTES

1. Sheldon Krantz, *The Legal Profession: What Is Wrong and How to Fix It* (New Providence, N.J.: LexisNexis, 2014), 3. See also Stephen M. Sheppard, "The American Legal Profession in the Twenty-First Century," *American Journal of Comparative Law* 62 (2014): 241–272 (arguing lawyers perform key functions and roles that are essential to American society).

2. Anthony Chase, "Lawyers and Popular Culture: A Review of Mass Media Portrayals of American Attorneys," *American Bar Foundation Research Journal* 11 (1986): 281, 284.

3. Lawrence M. Friedman, *A History of American Law*, 3rd ed. (New York, N.Y.: Touchstone, 2005), 53–59.

4. Martin Loughlin, "Judicial Independence and Judicial Review in Constitutional Democracies: A Note on Hamilton and Tocqueville," in *Effective Judicial Review: A Cornerstone of Good Governance*, ed. Christopher Forsyth, Mark Elliott, Swati Jhaveri, Michael Ramsden, and Anne Scully-Hill (New York, N.Y.: Oxford University Press, 2010), 9–18.

5. Krantz, *Legal Profession*.

6. Ibid., 1–2.

7. Deborah L. Rhode, *The Trouble with Lawyers* (New York, N.Y.: Oxford University Press, 2015); Benjamin H. Barton, *Glass Half Full: The Decline and Rebirth of the Legal Profession* (New York, N.Y.: Oxford University Press, 2015); William Domnarski, *Swimming in Deep Water: Lawyers, Judges, and Our Troubled Legal Profession* (Chicago, Ill.: American Bar Association, 2014); Steven J. Harper, *The Lawyer Bubble* (New York, N.Y.: Basic Books, 2013); James E. Moliterno, *The American Legal Profession in Crisis: Resistance and Responses to Change* (New York, N.Y.: Oxford University Press, 2010); Thomas D. Morgan, *The Vanishing Lawyer* (New York, N.Y.: Oxford University Press, 2010); Douglas Litowitz, *The Destruction of Young Lawyers: Beyond One L* (Akron, Ohio: University of Akron Press, 2006); Anthony Kronman, *The Lost Lawyer: Failing Ideals of the Legal Profession* (Cambridge, Mass.: Belknap Press of Harvard University Press, 1993).

8. Rhode, *Trouble with Lawyers*, 2.

9. Michael Asimow, "When Lawyers Were Heroes," *University of San Francisco Law Review* 30 (1996): 1131–1138.

10. Frederic S. Ury, "Saving Atticus Finch: The Lawyer and the Legal Services Revolution," in *The Relevant Lawyer: Reimagining the Future of the Legal Profession* (Chicago, Ill.: American Bar Association, 2015), 3–4.

11. Asimow, "When Lawyers Were Heroes," 1132.

12. Morgan, *Vanishing Lawyer*, 49–55.

13. Asimow, "When Lawyers Were Heroes," 1135–1137.

14. Ibid., 1133–1134.

15. Ibid., 1133.

16. Chase, "Lawyers and Popular Culture," 281.

17. Ibid., 284.

18. Marc Galanter, "The Faces of Mistrust: The Image of Lawyers in Public Opinion, Jokes, and Political Discourse," *University of Cincinnati Law Review* (1998): 805, 811.

19. Asimow, "When Lawyers Were Heroes," 1133; Marvin W. Mindes and Alan C. Acock, "Trickster, Hero, Helper: A Report on the Lawyer Image," *Law & Social Inquiry* 7 (1982): 180.

20. Domnarski, *Swimming in Deep Water*, 11. The "cursed Hungry Caterpillars" quote is in Christopher P. Banks and David M. O'Brien, *The Judicial Process: Law, Courts, and Judicial Politics* (Thousand Oaks, Calif.: Sage/CQ Press, 2015), 142.

21. Galanter, "Faces of Mistrust," 808.

22. Deborah L. Rhode, *In the Interests of Justice: Reforming the Legal Profession* (New York, N.Y.: Oxford University Press, 2000), 4.

23. Ibid., 3–8.
24. Galanter, "Faces of Mistrust," 810; Herbert M. Kritzer, *Lawyers at Work* (New Orleans, La.: Quid Pro Books, 2015), 269–270; American Tort Reform Foundation, *Judicial Hellholes 2016–2017*, accessed February 22, 2017, from www.judicialhellholes.org/wp-content/uploads/2016/12/JudicialHellholes-2016.pdf.
25. Rhode, *In the Interests of Justice*, 3, 6.
26. Robert Rubinson, "There Is No Such Thing as Litigation: Access to Justice and the Realities of Adjudication," *The Journal of Gender, Race & Justice* 18 (Winter 2015): 185–210.
27. Marc Galanter, "Reading the Landscape of Disputes: What We Know and Don't Know (and Think We Know) about Our Allegedly Contentious and Litigious Society," *University of California Los Angeles Law Review* 31 (1983): 4–71.
28. Kitty Calavita and Valerie Jenness, "Inside the Pyramid of Disputes: Naming Problems and Filing Grievances in California Prisons," *Social Problems* 60 (2013): 50–80; William Haltom and Michael McCann, *Distorting the Law: Politics, Media, and the Litigation Crisis* (Chicago, Ill.: University of Chicago Press, 2004); Marc Galanter, "Real World Torts: An Antidote to Anecdote," *Maryland Law Review* 55 (1996): 1094–1160; Richard E. Miller and Austin Sarat, "Grievances, Claims, and Disputes: Assessing the Adversary Culture," *Law and Society Review* 15 (1980–1981): 525–566; William L. F. Felstiner, Richard L. Abel, and Austin Sarat, "The Emergence and Transformation of Disputes: Naming, Blaming, and Claiming . . . ," *Law and Society Review* 15 (1980–1981): 631–654; Marc Galanter, "Access to Justice in a World of Expanding Social Capability," *Fordham Law Review* 38 (2010): 115–128.
29. Banks and O'Brien, *Judicial Process*, 208, 243.
30. Marc Galanter, "The Vanishing Trial: An Examination of Trials and Related Matters in Federal and State Courts," *Journal of Empirical Legal Studies* 1 (2004): 459–570.
31. Banks and O'Brien, *Judicial Process*, 271.
32. John H. Langbein, "The Disappearance of Civil Trial in the United States," *Yale Law Journal* 122 (2012): 533–534; Thomas J. Stipanowich, "ADR and the 'Vanishing Trial': The Growth and Impact of 'Alternative Dispute Resolution,'" *Journal of Empirical Legal Studies* (November 2004): 843, 849–850.
33. Lauren Ingeno, "The Upside of Law School," *Inside Higher Ed* (July 17, 2013), accessed August 3, 2016, from www.insidehighered.com/news/2013/07/17/report-shows-law-school-still-good-investment. See also Jennifer Cheeseman Day and Eric C. Newburger, "The Big Payoff: Educational Attainment and Synthetic Estimates of Work-Life Earnings," *Current Population Reports* (Washington, D.C.: U.S. Census Bureau, July 2002), accessed April 24, 2016, from www.census.gov/prod/2002pubs/p23-210.pdf.
34. Peter Taylor et al., *Is College Worth It? College Presidents, Public Assess Value, Quality and Mission of Higher Education* (Washington, D.C.: Pew Research Center Social & Demographic Trends, May 2011), 108–109, accessed April 24, 2016, from www.pewsocialtrends.org/files/2011/05/higher-ed-report.pdf.
35. U.S. Department of Labor, Bureau of Labor Statistics, "Employment Projections: Occupational Employment, Job Openings and Worker Characteristics," accessed April 24, 2016, from www.bls.gov/emp/ep_table_107.htm.
36. Harper, *Lawyer Bubble*, 4.
37. Brian Z. Tamanaha, *Failing Law Schools* (Chicago, Ill.: University of Chicago Press, 2012), 135.
38. Barton, *Glass Half Full*, 144–145.
39. Tamanaha, *Failing Law Schools*, 135.
40. Susan Swaim Diacoff, *Lawyer, Know Thyself: A Psychological Analysis of Personality Strengths and Weaknesses* (Washington, D.C.: American Psychological Association, 2004), 54.
41. Barton, *Glass Half Full*, 144.
42. Paul Campos, "Lawyers and Spoiled Identity," *Georgetown Journal of Legal Ethics* 28 (2014): 73–121.

43. Diacoff, *Lawyer, Know Thyself*, 51–56.

44. Harper, *Lawyer Bubble*, 4.

45. Diacoff, *Lawyer, Know Thyself*, 51–56; Barton, *Glass Half Full*, 146.

46. Harper, *Lawyer Bubble*, 5.

47. Tamanaha, *Failing Law Schools*, 135–136.

48. Harper, *Lawyer Bubble*, 5.

49. Ibid., 4–5.

50. Harper, *Lawyer Bubble*, 5; Tamanaha, *Failing Law Schools*, 138.

51. Tamanaha, *Failing Law Schools*, 138.

52. Ibid., 136.

53. Ibid., 136–137.

54. Herwig Schlunk, "Mamas 2011: Is a Law Degree a Good Investment Today?," *Journal of the Legal Profession* 36 (2011): 301–327.

55. Ibid., 327.

56. Deborah L. Rhode, *Access to Justice* (New York, N.Y.: Oxford University Press, 2004), 3.

57. Paul D. Carrington, *American Lawyers: Public Servants and the Development of a Nation* (Chicago, Ill.: American Bar Association, 2012), 9. See also Jason P. Nance and Paul E. Madsen, "An Empirical Analysis of Diversity in the Legal Profession," *Connecticut Law Review* 47 (2014): 271, 274.

58. Barton, *Glass Half Full*, 19.

59. Moliterno, *The American Legal Profession in Crisis*, 6. The quoted material is found in Friedman, *A History of American Law*, 227.

60. Moliterno, *The American Legal Profession in Crisis*, 18–21.

61. Ibid., 24.

62. Ibid., 24–45.

63. Ibid., 45.

64. Ibid., 18.

65. Kritzer, *Lawyers at Work*, 272–273.

66. Banks and O'Brien, *Judicial Process*, 121–125 (see Tables 4.2 and 4.3).

67. Rhode, *Trouble with Lawyers*, 61–74.

68. Nance and Madsen, "Diversity in the Legal Profession," 317–318.

2 Applying to Law School

Today, there are approximately 1.3 million lawyers in the United States. The legal profession is a $246 billion industry. There are over 169,000 legal establishments and 163,000 law offices across America. That translates into one lawyer for every 313 people living in the nation, a per capita rate that surpasses all other countries. Although the pace of U.S. legal practice has slowed and fewer students are going into law school than in past years, there are plenty of law schools to meet existing demand since there are over two hundred American Bar Association–accredited institutions in the United States. The rapid expansion of the Internet presents even more nonconventional distance learning options for legal training. In light of the sheer magnitude of the American legal profession, it is not surprising that legal scholar Mary Ann Glendon once quipped that we are truly a nation under lawyers.[1]

Taking stock of the current state of the American legal profession is important for anyone seriously contemplating law study and legal practice. As two legal researchers explain, "One cannot understand the functions of law in our society without understanding who lawyers are, who they represent, and what they do."[2] In that spirit, what follows is a thumbnail sketch of the profession in terms of information and issues that are important to know about in the early stages of thinking about a legal career and making the decision to apply to law school. The discussion first introduces students to the legal profession by giving an overview of contemporary legal education and the nature of law schools, lawyer demographics, legal practice settings, and the key issue of financing a legal education. Thereafter, the process of preparing for a law career is explained by analyzing prelaw undergraduate studies and some of the considerations that are significant in choosing a law school. The chapter concludes by briefly outlining the steps and implications of applying once the decision to go to law school is made.

A BRIEF INTRODUCTION TO THE AMERICAN LEGAL PROFESSION

In the United States, becoming a lawyer most often necessitates going to graduate school after completing a four-year undergraduate education. Ordinarily, but not exclusively, students opt to attend a law school that is accredited by the American Bar Association (ABA), the leading national organization of licensed lawyers. For a variety of reasons, a few students choose to attend a non-ABA-accredited law school or to secure a legal education by apprenticeship (law office study that may still require some law school training, depending on the jurisdiction) or, in Wisconsin, diploma privilege (bar admission after graduating from an in-state law school) (discussed in Chapter 3). After law school, graduates must be granted a professional license to practice law if that is their intention, a process that is controlled by state bar licensing authorities that are supervised by the state or jurisdiction's court of last resort.[3]

Law graduates do not need to pass the bar if they wish to engage in nonlegal employment, though many do anyway. One of the most useful aspects of getting a legal education is that it gives graduates a functional degree that inherently gives degree holders the flexibility to apply it to a wide range of law-related occupations as well as nonlegal vocations, including those in the public or private sectors such as government jobs or employment in business areas. Scholars thus observe that "[a] law degree . . . can open doors in politics, business, law enforcement, and other fields where clear thinking and a knowledge of our nation's laws is valued." Depending on a person's interests, strengths, and past work experience, employment opportunities within the law may be found in private law firms, corporate legal departments, and federal or state government positions. Outside of the law, law schools and law-related organizations tout the so-called JD Advantage, a shorthand description for suggesting that a law degree gives an edge over the competition in getting jobs that value legal training but do not require bar passage. In this light, a law degree may be an anchor or a complement to careers in human resources, education, health care, real estate, journalism, sports and entertainment, nonprofit advocacy, international relations, or community affairs.[4] A law degree, as well, has plenty of heft in making lateral changes within the legal profession or, alternatively, functions as a stepping-stone for switching careers entirely. The degree's utility is especially significant because job mobility and turnover are prevalent in the legal profession: one empirical study reports that 85 percent of mid-career lawyers changed jobs at least once, and half did so at least twice[5]; and analogous research discovered that there was frequent movement between jobs, organizations, and practice settings, and lawyers who had graduated only three years earlier changed employment at least once.[6]

Lawyer Demographics

In the fall of 2016, 351,201 1L (first-year) applicants sought law school admission to U.S. law schools. Of those, 145,312 were accepted, and 37,107 matriculated. Data sent to the American Bar Association from ABA-approved law schools indicate that there is a total of 110,951 students enrolled in juris doctor (JD) programs, an almost 3 percent decline from 2015. Although in recent years fewer students have been applying to law school, the rates of matriculation for 1L students are virtually the same for 2016 (37,107) and 2015 (37,071). Among matriculants, the rate of attrition roughly averages 6,400 per year (from 2008 to 2013). For those staying in school, the 2015 class graduated 39,984 law students who then entered into the workforce, a frequency that is consistent but slightly below recent past years.[7]

These numbers raise the issue of whether achieving a traditional legal education (one that contemplates passing a bar examination in order to secure employment) remains viable, an issue legal commentators and reformers have pressed in light of the 2008 economic downturn that severely constricted the legal economy. According to estimates, every year roughly forty thousand law graduates enter the market; but there are typically only about twenty-five thousand job openings for qualified applicants passing the bar. Therefore, the glutted legal marketplace necessitates that law students must be flexible in their mind-set and approach to employment; they should, for example, consider using their legal training in nontraditional ways that encompass taking positions in nonlegal fields, such as claims adjusting, risk or human resources management, and financial advising, or as city or town managers.[8] The growing interest in alternative nonlegal careers is discussed more fully in Chapter 4.

While the total number of lawyers remains high and the traditional use of their legal skills remains uncertain, it is noteworthy that most attorneys concentrate their practice in mostly urban areas across only six states and one territory: New York (175,195), California (167,690), Texas (87,957), Florida (75,697), Illinois (63,060), Pennsylvania (49,644), and the District of Columbia (52,711).[9] Although women are increasingly entering the legal profession, the gains made in gender representation are only a relatively recent phenomenon. On balance, the legal profession is homogeneous and unrepresentative. Women, as well as minorities and individuals with disabilities, face considerable equal employment challenges as well as workplace inequities. For example, by virtually every metric, male lawyers dominate legal practice not only in terms of sheer numbers, but also in holding higher-paying jobs and leadership positions in law firms, Fortune 500 companies, law school administration, and the judiciary (see Table 2.1).

Moreover, the National Association for Law Placement reported that (1) 8 percent of minorities in law firms were partners, whereas 20 percent were employed as associate attorneys, in 2015; (2) 3 percent or less of openly lesbian, gay, bisexual, and transgender (LGBT) lawyers worked in law firms, either as partners or as associates, in 2015; and (3) less than half of 1 percent of lawyers were disabled partners or associate attorneys in 2015. According to one study, the discrepancies in representation, compensation, and implicitly professional influence are higher in the legal profession as compared to the medical, business, and academic professions.[10]

Table 2.1 Women and the Legal Profession

Metric	Female	vs.	Male
Women in the Legal Profession	36%		65%
Women in Private Practice			
• Summer Associates	48%		52%
• Associates	45%		55%
• Managing Partners in 200 Largest Law Firms	18%		82%
• Equity Partners	18%		82%
• Partners	22%		78%
Women in Corporations			
• Fortune 500 General Counsel	24%		76%
• Fortune 501–1000	19%		81%

(Continued)

Table 2.1   (Continued)

Metric	Female	vs.	Male
Women in Law School Administration			
• Deans	31%		69%
Women in Federal Courts			
• U.S. Supreme Court	33%		67%
• U.S. Courts of Appeals	35%		65%
• U.S. District Courts	33%		67%
Women in State Courts			
• Appellate Courts of Last Resort	35%		65%
• Intermediate Appellate Courts	35%		65%
• Trial Courts of General Jurisdiction	30%		70%
• Trial Courts of Limited Jurisdiction	33%		67%
Women lawyers' median weekly salary as a percentage of male lawyers' salary (2014)	83% ($1,590 vs. $1,915)		—
Women equity partner compensation in the 200 largest firms as compared to male partner (October 2015 report)	80% (30 firms supplied data)		—

Source: American Bar Association, Commission on Women in the Profession, "A Current Glance at Women in the Law: May 2016," accessed May 4, 2016, from www.americanbar.org/content/dam/aba/marketing/women/current_glance_statistics_may2016.authcheckdam.pdf.

Note: All percentages are subject to rounding error, so column and row totals may equal 100.

Legal Practice Settings

According to the National Association for Law Placement, 51 percent of almost forty thousand law graduates in 2015 found work in private practice, whereas the remainder secured employment in business (17 percent), government (12 percent), judicial clerkship (10 percent), public interest (7 percent), or academic (2 percent) jobs.[11] Another study investigating thousands of attorneys who were in practice for twelve years mostly mirrors these employment trends: nearly 50 percent of lawyers still worked in private law firms, but 28 percent moved on to the public sector while 20 percent remained in business settings.[12] For graduates landing a job in private practice, over 50 percent worked in small law firms of twenty-five or fewer attorneys. In Big Law corporate firms, 23 percent were placed in firms with over five hundred lawyers. For firms with fewer than five hundred lawyers, the percentages were largely identical across large to medium-size firms: 6 percent in firms with 251–500 lawyers; 6 percent in firms with 101–250 lawyers; 5 percent in firms with 51–100 lawyers; and 6 percent in firms with 26–50 lawyers. For smaller firms,

10 percent landed in 11- to 25-lawyer–sized firms, and 40 percent were in firms with 10 or fewer lawyers. In contrast, only 4 percent reported entering into solo practice. These figures underscore other research findings that debunk the popular belief that most attorneys in private practice wind up in Big Law firms. Most simply do not. These demographics help mask but also exemplify the reality that earning a law degree is *not* a guarantee of employment, at least right after law school, especially in a large law firm. For the 2015 class, 4,224 lawyers, or 11 percent of law graduates, were unemployed or not seeking a job. As a result, many new graduates (especially in nonelite schools) struggle to find a job because the supply for entry-level positions far outpaces demand, a trend that has been exacerbated by the negative economic consequences of the 2008 recession. As legal scholar Deborah L. Rhode puts it, "there is a mismatch between supply and demand" because the "number of new law graduates substantially outstrips the entry-level jobs that are available."[13]

Furthermore, the legal profession workplace is highly stratified and extremely specialized, especially in private practice settings. In the past, legal practice was divided along class and religious segments; but, more recently, some studies have observed that changing racial attitudes, the entry of women into the legal profession, and the growing competition for hiring the best associate attorney talent have slowed the pace of stratification and, arguably, made professional advancement hinge more on considerations of individual merit. In addition, and contrary to popular belief, most lawyers are not generalists or equipped to handle any legal problem with ease. In fact, the opposite is true. As one law professor explains, "new lawyers are prepared to handle very little and more experienced lawyers focus on narrow areas of practice." In this respect, law practice is "so highly specialized that most lawyers, out of necessity, have to restrict their areas of practices." Thus, as their professional career unfolds, many lawyers develop specialties that take them into well-defined areas of criminal law, international law, family law, tax law, employment law, sports law, education law, and the like.[14]

Moreover, savvy law applicants or students quickly perceive that their chances for achieving the best professional success (in terms of money, influence, and status in the community or profession) may pivot on finding a job in Big Law, or large corporate law firms that offer the type of resources and networking that enable driven professionals to maximize their pedigree and skills. Yet landing a high-powered job generally depends on several factors, including social pedigree (most matriculating law students are from upper-middle-class to middle-class socioeconomic status), the prestige of the law school from which a graduate is hired, and, perhaps most significantly, how well the student performed in law school. Social pedigree, once a dominant factor in explaining career outcomes, has perhaps become less influential as the legal profession has become more diversified since the mid-1990s. Consequently, *where* one goes to law school, and *how well* one does in law school, probably determine a lawyer's career path and whether fledging attorneys land in Big Law firms or otherwise find lucrative professional positions. As one empirical study concludes, "'who you are' has declined in importance as a determinant of legal careers, and 'what you do' matters more. What students show they can do in law school—at *all* law schools—is very closely linked to both their short-term and long-term career success." Still, not landing in a top-tier school has its quality-of-life advantages because many lawyers are extremely satisfied and personally happy in their choice to attend less renowned schools since their employment puts fewer demands on their time and is less stressful.[15]

Regardless, common sense and many academic studies indicate that graduates from prestigious law schools are more likely to wind up in large law firms, whereas students from less distinguished schools are relegated to mid-size to small law firms. The elitism of law study—which traditionally has been closely tied to the applicant's social origins—registers that admission to law school, and the law training process itself, stratifies attorneys into "haves and have-nots" classifications that inevitably factor into job placement trends and whether new lawyers find themselves in the best position to reap tangible and intangible professional rewards as their careers progress. As one legal scholar ironically observes, Big Law "firms do have a disproportionate amount of power both within and outside the legal profession even though they comprise a relatively small percent of the lawyers in America."[16] Not surprisingly, an empirical study tracking the careers of elite and nonelite lawyers determined that the wage gap, which is quite substantial between the two groups, "begins the moment that lawyers start out the gate, and persists over time."[17]

Apart from private practice, only a small percentage of lawyers take public interest jobs or become judges or law teachers. Fewer law graduates pursue nonlegal careers, and sometimes only by necessity. In this regard, a large percentage of law graduates find positions in the business sector, and oftentimes being a licensed lawyer is not a job requirement. Having a law degree, though, is a plus (if not a necessity) for finding work in nontraditional employment settings, such as with online legal service companies like LegalZoom and Practical Law, or, alternatively, in lobbying, accounting, and management consulting firms. These employment trends are discussed in more detail in Chapter 4.[18]

Lawyer Salaries

The starting salaries of law graduates are variable and contingent upon the nature of employment, economic conditions, and where employment is secured.[19] In general terms, data from the National Association for Law Placement (NALP) provide a broad sense of historical trends and salary variation. Between 2008 and 2015, the median starting salary for lawyers declined from $72,000 to $64,800, a by-product of the Great Recession. In 2008, the law firm median starting salary was $125,000; but, in 2015, it was $100,000. Furthermore, salaries are commensurate with the bigness of the law firm because working in larger firms results in increased earning capacity. Median salaries have also grown over time. In 1995, the median starting salary of first-year associates was $45,000 for lawyers in 2- to 25-attorney firms; $50,000 (26–50 attorneys); $59,500 (51–100 attorneys); $58,500 (101–250 attorneys); and $70,000 (251 or more attorneys). By 2014, it was $68,000 (2–25 attorneys); $105,000 (26–50 attorneys); $110,000 (51–100 attorneys); $105,000 (101–250 attorneys); and $135,000 (251 or more attorneys).[20]

While being cognizant of reports of average or median salaries is important, what the numbers purport to represent must be weighed against the problems associated with unreported data, inflationary trends, or other marketplace nuances. In the spirit of full disclosure, some nonprofit organizations try to present a more accurate picture by publishing salaries and other employment outcome data that are reported from law graduates at specific schools; for example, Law School

Transparency publishes these data in its online "LST Score Reports."[21] In addition, NALP reports, along with other academic studies, show that lawyer salaries today are best understood in a bimodal distribution; that is, "salaries cluster at either side of the average," and "relatively few salaries are near the average" in most recent years. For the 2014 class, the distribution of salaries fell with two general "peak" ranges relative to Big Law positions and the balance of law graduates. About 17 percent of jobs paid $160,000, whereas about half of reported salaries were in the $40,000–$65,000 range.[22] Other scholars, as well, have interpreted the NALP data in similar terms while underscoring that since 2006, the salary "gap between the Big Law humps and everyone else is extremely pronounced," a circumstance that implies that "[a] student who hoped to work at a big law firm and ends up in a small firm will be disappointed indeed."[23]

Another consideration in weighing lawyer salaries is that the competition for the best new attorney talent is fierce, especially in the private practice sector. In 2016, an elite law firm, Cravath, Swaine & Moore, announced that it was raising the annual salary for its first-year recruits from $160,000 to $180,000, a move that put pressure on other Big Law firms to follow suit lest they lose a chance to hire the nation's best law graduates. Yet the salary adjustment is the first increase to high-powered associate pay in over a decade, and it comes amid the growing recognition by elite law firms that they can no longer afford to let deep-pocket but disgruntled clients absorb the costs of delegating high-priced legal work to junior associates. The change in behavior allowed partner profits to rise and made the pay increase possible once more experienced attorneys in the firm handled the high-producing revenue files. Notably, though, if other elite law firms decide to match the pay increase, it only applies to a small percentage of the legal industry. Only a few law graduates begin their careers with mid-$100,000 starting salaries.[24]

Furthermore, where one finds work is significant. Apart from law firms, the median salaries of 2015 graduates were higher in the business and industry sector ($70,000) but lower in the government ($55,000), academic ($50,000), and public interest ($47,000) employment settings.[25] While some lawyers undoubtedly earn big paychecks, it is worth bearing in mind that many do not. Compared to past years, income levels are generally declining, in part due to competitive pressures. Some observers, in fact, go so far as equating lawyers' earnings to those working in other lower-salaried professional callings, such as high school teachers ($53,230), accountants and auditors ($61,690), architects ($72,550), and civil engineers ($77,560).[26]

Student Loan Debt

Another (but not the last or only) consideration in evaluating the current state of the legal profession relates to the specter of paying back student loan debts, whether they are accumulated in undergraduate or law school, or both. Clearly, the cost of attending law school has to be carefully weighed against the remunerative (and intangible) benefits of earning a legal education. Making that assessment has to be done in light of the reality of high tuition rates and the cost of attendance in a contemporary legal marketplace that is not always a predictable or reliable source of employment. Not all students need to finance their education, but many do.

Students not considering the issue beforehand are often shocked to learn how expensive it is to attend graduate school. There is little doubt that tuition rates have skyrocketed in the past thirty years. In 1985, the median tuition rate for public law schools was $1,792 for residents and $4,786 for nonresidents; for private schools, it was $7,385. By 2013, it grew to $22,209 for residents going to public schools and $33,752 for nonresidents. And, for private schools, it rose to $42,241.[27] Beyond the tuition rate, the cost of attendance (which typically includes living expenses, such as room and board, fees, books and supplies, transportation, and miscellaneous personal expenses) must be factored into the calculation of whether it is wise or necessary to assume student loan debt. According to the American Bar Association, for single students living on campus, the average cost of living and book expenses rose from roughly $5,000 per year in 1990 to $15,000 by 2012–2013[28]; and, at a minimum, students financing their legal education will borrow between an average of about $85,000 (for public law schools) and $122,000 (for private law schools) over the course of their study, or an average of about $32,000 (public) to $44,000 (private) per year.[29] In all likelihood, as the nonprofit entity Law School Transparency indicates, the ABA's data underestimate the true cost of attendance because going to law school entails incurring a variety of expenses, and opportunity costs, that are not easily foreseen without advance, and diligent, investigation by prospective students.[30]

The lingering impact of educational debt, and how it affects a level of professional satisfaction (or regret) that is felt over time, is perhaps the most critical factor in deciding whether to go law school. In a national longitudinal study of several thousand U.S. law graduates who were admitted into the bar in 2000, researchers reported that 47 percent had zero educational debt after twelve years of legal practice and that only 5 percent had $100,000 (or more) of debt remaining at the end of that time. But the findings also showed that lawyers working in law firms with 101–249 or over 250 attorneys were the most likely to have paid down their debt entirely and that although certain lawyers, such as those in public interest, nonprofit, education, and federal government jobs, successfully paid off educational debt, lawyers in solo practice, state government, legal services, or public defender positions struggled and were the least likely to do so. In addition, after twelve years of legal practice, the median debt was roughly $50,000; but, significantly, that educational debt was harder to pay off and lingered more for blacks, Hispanics, and Asians (but not whites).[31]

The decision to assume student loan debt is further complicated by other intangibles and realities that are an integral part of the law school admission process. Law schools, for example, offer internal grants in aid, scholarships, and tuition discounts that may be awarded to students, depending on how their application and underlying credentials are weighed by the admission committee. Due to the competitive pressures of enrollment and the law school ranking system (discussed later in this chapter), oftentimes less renowned or nonelite schools use these tools as a recruitment incentive in the hopes of attracting better students and graduates who, in time, may improve the school's reputation. A controversial incentive, such as conditional scholarships, may be offered at the time of admission: thus, a student is given a financial award, but it is conditioned and retained only if the student maintains a certain grade point average or class standing (other than remaining in good academic standing). Criticizing these as "bait and switch" tactics, the American Bar Association now mandates that accredited law schools must disclose, through so-called Standard 509 Information Reports, whether they offer conditional scholarships and, if so, how many have been lost due to the inability to fulfill the conditions for retaining awards (and therefore students must find other means to pay tuition to stay in school, like student loans).[32]

Finally, for those taking on educational debt, students are most likely to take out loans from the federal government, such as Stafford Loans or Direct PLUS Loans, or from private lenders such as Citizens Bank, Social Finance (SoFi), or Common Bond. While some students opt for private lenders (which have more rigid payment terms and less forbearance flexibility), many students choose loans from the federal government because it offers a variety of repayment options based on income or other factors that assist with paying down debt; or, in some instances, loan forgiveness programs are in place to erase some or all of the debt that is accumulated after a period of time. That option is available for certain types of post–law school employment, such as working in public interest or teaching organizations.[33] Even so, and although students with limited means may be able to subsidize most if not all of their legal education, critics observe that repaying large loan amounts is often very difficult, if not "crippling," simply because more than 40 percent of law graduates will not make enough money in their first position to service the debt adequately.[34]

PREPARING FOR LAW SCHOOL: "PRELAW" UNDERGRADUATE STUDIES

Aspiring lawyers must approach the task of preparing for law school with a "seriousness of purpose" and a keen ability to make the necessary time investment to gather, and carefully evaluate, relevant information about the law school admission process and what it takes to be successful and happy after matriculation and bar passage. Prelaw students must keep a detached, objective, and critical eye on the self-assessment process in order to be in the best position to "yield lifetime rewards and avoid enduring mistakes."[35] Since studies show that matriculating students overestimate their success in law school, it is logical to think that the same mistake is likely to happen if unrealistic choices are made about where to send applications (it will also be a costly error, as applying to law school is not especially cheap). A key player in law school admissions, the Law School Admission Council (discussed later), reminds students that roughly half of applicants apply to five or fewer schools, a metric suggesting that many enrollees are thoughtfully taking into account a wide range of personal and academic considerations before applying; but, still, the rest apparently are not as careful.[36] Clearly, critical decisions that affect a lifetime should only be made after students fully understand the pros and cons of applying to law school and becoming a legal professional. After discussing what type of undergraduate or prelaw study is beneficial to law school preparation, this section analyzes some of the practical considerations and logistics of applying to, and choosing, the best law school.

Prelaw Undergraduate Study

A common misconception is that there is a recommended undergraduate curriculum for law school—one that "best" prepares students for law study. The American Bar Association, as well as the Law School Admission Council (a key resource for learning about law study, the law school application process, and lawyering), does not recommend students choose any specific undergraduate majors or group of courses to prepare for a legal education.[37] In reality, there is no "prelaw" degree; instead, schools typically subsume their prelaw programs into another degree. In this context, many students elect to major in political science (or take a healthy dose of poli-sci courses) because it gives students a special grounding in understanding American government, legal institutions, and the judicial process (see Table 2.2). This common-sense approach to prelaw studies is echoed by legal reformers who argue that judicial or legal process courses, with others that introduce students to the law, legal reasoning, legal systems, and the legal profession, must be structured into prelaw prerequisites that are enforceable through ABA accreditation standards and, perhaps, passing a qualifying examination. Establishing prerequisites and compelling a prelaw qualifying examination would help students decide their career path as well as filter out unqualified applicants. Even so, until reform is enacted, the unstructured curriculum norm in prelaw studies puts the onus on students to determine what undergraduate courses will best prepare them for the rigors of graduate school and legal training.

As Table 2.2 indicates, many law school applicants predominantly major in political science but also gravitate toward majoring in subjects within liberal arts disciplines. Other traditional options that the ABA lists for law preparation include history, English, philosophy, economics, and business majors or courses; but it adds that law students ultimately come from a diverse and fairly open-ended range of undergraduate backgrounds from art and music to science, mathematics, and engineering. This latter ABA observation is consistent with an empirical study's finding that science, technology, engineering, and math (STEM) and economics, accounting, and finance (EAR) majors are especially useful predictors of law school success. Further, law professor Derek Muller's research similarly reports that certain majors, among them physics, math, art history, and linguistics, are near the top of a pool of majors that earned high undergraduate grade-point average (UGPA) and Law School Admission Test (LSAT) scores, and that classics, math, linguistics, art history, physics, philosophy, and economics majors had the best UGPA and LSAT scores among law school matriculants.[38] While there is no guarantee that declaring those types of majors will lead to law admission or law school grade accomplishment, students must strive to do well in any major they choose, and not only take courses that are intellectually challenging but also hone analytical reasoning, oral communication, and writing skills. Being diligent academically, moreover, will also pay off for students who can take advantage of 3+3 programs if they are offered by a student's undergraduate institution. Such programs permit undergraduates to apply to and begin law school after three years, if certain requirements are met. Upon completion of the first year in law school, the applicant graduates from the undergraduate level and then completes the second and third years of law school, which has the effect reducing the overall years (and costs) of academic study.[39]

In weighing the different options, students often seek information from the undergraduate institution's prelaw adviser, who may be a part of a specific academic program (e.g., prelaw, legal, or paralegal studies) or more generically located in the administrative structure of university or college advising offices or specific departments. Prelaw advisers help identify relevant law-related resources and assist advisees in the application process. Typically, they provide guidance in suggesting relevant coursework and supply key information about how to register for the

Table 2.2   Most Popular Undergraduate Majors for Law School
Applicants, 2015–2016

Rank	Major	Total Applicants	Number Enrolled	Percentage Enrolled
1	Political Science	12,693	9,030	71.14%
2	Criminal Justice	3,857	2,106	54.60%
3	Psychology	3,778	2,564	67.87%
4	English	3,549	2,437	68.67%
5	History	3,472	2,561	73.76%
6	Economics	2,717	1,943	71.51%
7	Philosophy	2,294	1,736	75.68%
8	Arts & Humanities	2,135	1,444	67.63%
9	Sociology	2,055	1,266	61.61%
10	Communications	1,809	1,195	60.06%
11	Business Administration	1,554	850	54.70%
12	Finance	1,468	980	66.76%
13	Liberal Arts	1,311	775	59.12%
14	Business Management	1,085	624	57.51%
15	International Relations	1,026	754	73.49%
16	Accounting	962	561	58.32%
17	Criminology	931	562	60.37%
18	Spanish	906	659	72.74%
19	Marketing	902	591	65.52%
20	Biology, General	744	497	66.80%

Source: Law School Admission Council, "Applicants by Major: Undergraduate Majors of Applicants to ABA-Approved Law Schools," accessed August 5, 2016, from www.lsac.org/lsacresources/data/applicants-by-major.

LSAT, the Law School Admission Council (LSAC), and the Credential Assembly Service, as well as aid students in completing the online application process. Prelaw advisers are a good resource for learning how to apply for financial aid, and often they supervise or work with prelaw clubs, undergraduate moot court or mock trial programs, and law firms or organizations that have internships. A prelaw adviser may also have key contacts or ongoing relationships with law schools and law-related alumni, which gives students the chance to attend law school recruiting events or develop a network of professional resources that cannot be obtained or gleaned through online resources.[40]

Regardless of the chosen major, in selecting coursework it is advantageous for students to opt for challenging courses that help develop the types of skills that are linked to being a lawyer or the legal profession itself. The ABA-LSAC identifies seven basic skills that lawyers use in the practice of law: reading and listening, analyzing, synthesizing (the law), advocating, counseling, writing and speaking, and negotiating. Although lawyers may use some skills more than others, the legal training they receive establishes the foundation they need to analyze legal issues relative to the law's current state, and thus to advise clients appropriately about what the law requires and how it may affect them in the case at hand or in the future. In addition, lawyers play different roles in the delivery of legal services, so the skills they acquire must include learning how to negotiate and advocate positions well and to communicate lucidly in a written and oral fashion.[41]

This prelaw advice reinforces the notion that the skill set that ought to be developed at the undergraduate level is cultivated by courses that allow students to refine their abilities to engage in problem solving, critical thinking, research, writing, and oral communication. As a result, coursework that exposes students to American politics, American political thought (and constitutional history), the judicial process, sociology, financial analysis, business management, philosophy, literature, ethics, and international relations is typically a good foundation for law study. With these types of courses, prelaw students establish a solid grounding in not only abstract concepts of human behavior; historical, societal, or cultural development; and general politics, but also practical skills of mathematics and business acumen.[42]

On another dimension, students should be cognizant of taking courses that expose them to college-level (or life) experiences that cultivate an awareness that the practice of law is a *profession*, and one that has clear expectations and obligations about how to act appropriately in rendering legal services. Learning professional competence is essential because lawyers are routinely asked to make difficult choices about how to give objective, and emotionally detached, advice to clients who are often in a crisis mode and cannot think too clearly about the situation at hand. While it may be too much to expect that undergraduate prelaw studies can adequately familiarize students with the values underlying legal professionalism (after all, in theory, that is what law schools should be doing), it is never too early to begin to develop a mind-set in college that prepares students for the types of advising and transactional lawyering roles they are likely to assume in legal practice. In this respect, prelaw students should develop a curriculum that trains them to learn how to remain ethical in legal practice; to become effective listeners, communicators, investigators, advocates, problem solvers, and advisers; and, in the twenty-first century, to become proficient in using relevant and rapidly evolving technologies.[43]

Beyond coursework, many students interested in law consult a wide range of books that reveal what it is like to go to law school, be a lawyer, and work in the legal profession. For students who do not personally know a lawyer or have a relative in the legal profession, working through a prelaw book list—which might include learning what Harvard Law School is like from Scott Turow's *One L* or reading about the litigation history behind the landmark case *Brown v. Board of Education* (1954) in Richard Kluger's *Simple Justice*—is invaluable because it provides special insights about the law that cannot be learned in college courses.[44] These resources, as well, can be read in conjunction with taking part in internships (if offered during undergraduate study) or informal discussions with legal professionals and law school alumni about their own experiences in the law and the legal profession as a whole. Once a general familiarity of the law and legal practice is gained, then prelaw students must decide to prepare for and take the LSAT, a key element of the law school admission process.

The Law School Admission Test

A precondition for attending an ABA-accredited law school is performing well on the Law School Admission Test (LSAT). While the test can be taken after college, in many instances students begin to prepare for it in the last two years of their undergraduate education. Along with earning a strong UGPA, doing well on the LSAT is essential even though law schools purport to take a holistic approach to making law school admission decisions. As one law school dean explains, UGPA and LSAT scores are significant, but "they are only one of several pieces of the law school application puzzle." In this respect, admissions committees weigh all parts of the application, and the importance of any factor that determines an admission or denial "depend[s] on the strengths and weaknesses of the application as a whole."[45] Such factors include undergraduate curriculum and college attended, graduate work, grade improvement and grade distribution, extracurricular activities, ethnic or racial background, individual character and personality traits, letters of recommendation, writing skills, personal statement, work experience or other postundergraduate experiences, community activities or volunteer work, impetus and reason for wanting to study law, state of residency, any obstacles that have been surpassed, past accomplishments and leadership capacity, conditional admissions programs, and other distinctive aspects of the application.[46]

Contrary to popular belief, the LSAT does not test a person's substantive knowledge of the law. Rather, the LSAT is highly significant as an admission metric because its primary function is to evaluate the likelihood of an applicant's success in law school through testing an ability to perform the type of skills that lawyers routinely use in their legal practice. These include reading comprehension; managing, synthesizing, and making inferences from complex information and legal materials; critical thinking; and analyzing logical arguments. In terms of format, the LSAT is a multiple-choice test that consists of five 35-minute sections (four of which are scored), with a 35-minute unscored writing sample that is taken at the end of the exam (which is not scored, but forwarded to law schools where applications are sent). The multiple-choice design has three question types: reading comprehension, analytical reasoning, and logical reasoning. Whereas the reading comprehension section features three long and two short comparative reading passages, the analytical reasoning part has four logic games and short arguments, respectively.[47]

The LSAT score is generated from the number of correct answers, with no deduction for wrong answers. Individual questions are not weighted differently either. The lowest score is 120, and the highest is 180. After the test, the LSAC compiles an

LSAT Score Report, which includes the results of all tests (up to twelve) for which an applicant registered since June 1, 2011 (including absences and cancellations). Students ordinarily cannot take the LSAT more than three times in a two-year period, though the LSAC may grant exceptions. If there is more than one reportable score on record, the LSAT Score Report averages them but also lists them separately. Further, the report includes a percentile rank, or the percentage of LSAT takers whose scores were lower than the applicant's in question in the preceding three testing years. Test takers can expect their LSAT Score Reports to be received by email within three to four weeks following the test.[48]

While the LSAT is offered in four possible test months (June, September, December, and February), the most popular time to take the LSAT is in June or September of the year before the law school start date. For students engaged in foreign study, the test can be taken abroad, and there are alternative test days to accommodate religious observance. Taking the LSAT earlier will afford more time to prepare the law school applications, a time-consuming process in and of itself, especially if applicants are still in undergraduate school. As the LSAC notes, many law schools mandate that the LSAT be taken by December at the very latest to qualify for the next fall admission cycle. In order to take the LSAT, students must follow the procedures to register for it, a process that requires not only an investment of time but also the payment of fees by the appropriate deadlines. The first step for registration is to create an LSAC account (https://os.lsac.org/Release/Logon/Access.aspx), which permits LSAT registration and access to other LSAC services, such as the LSAC Credential Assembly Service (CAS; a onetime documentation submission procedure that lets the LSAC forward to each law school transcripts, letters of recommendation, and other credentials, instead of applicants doing it piecemeal by themselves), early notification of LSAT scores, buying test preparation materials, and attending LSAC-sponsored Law School Forums (recruiting events). Virtually all ABA-approved law schools require that applicants register for the LSAT *and* the CAS, so applicants should be mindful of and familiarize themselves with all of the basic and auxiliary fees associated with LSAC services. For 2016–2017, the basic fees for LSAT registration totaled $180, and the CAS cost $175. Other miscellaneous auxiliary fees include filing law school reports ($30), late registration ($90), test center or date changes ($90 each), hand scoring ($100), and the like. Under certain limited conditions, the LSAC permits fee waivers.[49]

Regardless of when the LSAT is taken, it is sound advice for students to only take it after sufficient and thorough preparation leading up to the test date. Although some studies report that LSAT scores predict law school success more weakly than having a strong UGPA, there is little doubt that high LSAT scores figure predominantly into admission committee decision making. Research, on balance, shows that the LSAT is a relatively reliable measurement of law school performance. Lower scores (those typically under 150) will have to be offset (and explained) by other positive elements of the application, such as a high UGPA or significant contribution to the community through volunteer work and the like. As a rule of thumb, because the test is so critical to the application process, students should take it under an assumption that their best score will happen after taking it only once. While the test can be retaken, it is costlier and time-consuming to do so, and there is no guarantee that the score will improve.[50]

There are basically two ways to prepare for the test (either in-person or online): through self-help (using commercial preparatory books that are available from the LSAC) or by using a commercial test preparation service (that has a combination of online, in-class, and personal tutoring options). In terms of self-help, the LSAC and other vendors give online access to sample test questions (and test preparation videos) and the chance to buy practice tests at a fairly minimal cost. While neither method is foolproof or a guarantee of success, the self-study option is the most cost-effective and most helpful for those who have not used a commercial test preparation service in the past for other types of standardized testing that are required for academic admissions. The commercial test preparation alternative may work better for students who need more structure and guided assistance to their study; also, such courses are beneficial resources for learning techniques to identify question types and strategies to solve them that are put into practice by the instructors—something that might not be achieved from self-study. Yet, they can be expensive and in some instances cost-prohibitive, as prices typically range in the hundreds to thousands of dollars. In weighing the decision to pay for commercial test preparation services, it is advisable for prelaw students to take some practice tests initially and then, when ready, take a timed test under mock testing conditions at least a few times. If the mock test scores are poor or in need of improvement, then using a commercial test preparation vendor may be a wise choice (with, of course, no guarantee of improvement or an acceptable LSAT score). Regardless of the chosen method, it is almost foolhardy to believe that a respectable LSAT performance will result from the poor decision to begin preparing for it at the last minute or close to the time the test is first taken. Only familiarity and a complete understanding of the test directions, test format, time constraints, and test-taking strategies through much practice will maximize the test results, something that typically takes a fair to large investment of time and plenty of hard work.[51]

Selecting the "Right" Law School

Once preparation for the LSAT has begun, and if they already have not done so, students should start to investigate what law school options are available to them in light of their personal circumstances, expectations, and goals about entering the legal profession or receiving law-based training. Of course, the actual decision to attend a specific school probably will not be made until the end of the application process or after the first acceptance letter arrives. Further, the choice about where to attend is made easier by economic, job, or family necessities or the fact that one may opt to go to a particular school because of limited acceptances to first preferences or a spate of denials that limit choice.[52] Nonetheless, searching for the "right" law school early on in the process (whether in undergraduate school or not) has the advantage of gathering key facts that is a natural (and indispensable) part not only of the self-examination process, but also of making an informed—and "best"—choice when the time comes. After all, as one legal scholar puts it in explaining the significance of making the right selection, "[n]ot only will the choice influence the next three years of your life, but it may also very well determine what type of law you practice, how you practice it, and how much you enjoy being a lawyer."[53]

The process of choosing a law school can only be accomplished by a thorough examination of the law schools themselves. An often cost-effective and convenient resource for learning about law schools is LSAC's Law School Forums, events that are attended by multiple law schools at regional locations across the nation for the purpose of educating students about the law school admission process.[54] One of the first steps in doing research about law schools is to determine if an institution is ABA accredited, as that is often a requirement to sit for a state bar examination.[55] Relatedly, appropriate thought must be given to identifying the location where the practice of law is likely to commence. While law degrees in and of themselves are quite functional and relatively portable across states (and sometimes bar passage is not required for employment, as noted earlier), it is often helpful to select a law school that is linked to the likely location of law practice, simply because law schools may help bar passage by having a state-friendly curriculum, access to resources, or other "in state" advantages that facilitate bar study or bar passage within a state. As well, the applicant's personal circumstances may necessitate living close to family, friends, or legal contacts that are gained in the course of growing up or living in the area for an extended period of time. While it is not always the case, it may be difficult for students who attend law school in California to do well in sitting for a bar examination in New York. What was taught and emphasized in California law schools over the course of three years—and what was learned during that time about that state's judicial system, rules of court, and substantive state law—might not be especially useful in trying to understand, and apply, similar information that is essential to know in passing the New York state bar examination. Virtually all bar examinations have components that test the familiarity and application of legal procedures and laws that are unique to the legal practice in the state. Accordingly, carefully thinking about where the bar will be taken probably should be part of the reasoning about where to attend law school.

Researching what law schools have to offer can be accomplished by reviewing individual law school websites that are available for review by the LSAC (www.lsac .org) and from the law schools themselves. The LSAC provides a full range of information, services, and programs relating to the legal profession and law schools (including, as mentioned earlier, law school recruitment forums, but also applicant profile grids, an online tool that is tailored to identifying law schools based on applicant UGPAs and LSAT scores). Also, the LSAC administers the LSAT and hosts a credentialing and candidate referral service that is part of the admissions process. The online tools supplied by the LSAC should be used in conjunction with taking a more detailed look at what each law school has to offer, a task that is easily accomplished by accessing the school's webpages.[56]

In reviewing these sites, students discover there are a variety of law school typologies, ranging from the *size* of the law school; to being educated in an institution from a public, private, independent, or faith-based perspective; to the law school's *location*, among others. Size and location are often critical factors, especially from undergraduates coming from smaller (or larger) school environments who have become accustomed to certain lifestyles or expectations in academic life. In general, there are several standard criteria to use in investigating specific schools, including the size, composition, and diversity of the student body; the location, size, and nature of the surrounding community; the law school's curriculum; the general atmosphere of the school; the availability of housing; the pedigree and expertise of the faculty; whether clinical programs or classroom experience is emphasized; the offerings of the library and the professionalism of the staff who manage them; whether there is a part-time or evening program; the track record and competence of career services; the nature of any specialty or joint-degree programs offered; and what types of law review, honor (i.e., Order of the Coif), moot court, or other law-related organizations (i.e., chapters from the Federalist Society or similar advocacy groups) are available as extracurricular activities.[57]

As a recent innovation, another source of key consumer information—the ABA Standard 509 Information Reports, mentioned earlier (www.abarequireddisclo sures.org)—compels law schools to reveal a wide range of data that help aspiring law students evaluate schools before they apply. By reviewing the reports, students can learn about a school's public or private status; admissions and enrollment data (including UGPA and LSAT scoring percentiles); incoming class demographics; tuition rates, financial aid, and the cost of attendance; grants and scholarships, including whether they are conditional (i.e., only remain in place if academic standards are met and, if not, are revoked or diminished); curriculum (including practice-ready or clinical courses), class size, and attrition rates; postgraduation employment data; and bar passage rates. As the LSAC recommends, students also should weigh other key variables, such as the school's location, full- and part-time study availability, faculty, library facilities, clinical programs, student organizations and journals, and whether there are any special programs (joint graduate degrees, such as JD/MBA, or one-year graduate Master of Laws [LLM] degrees that can be pursued after graduation). Beyond these considerations, in researching law schools carefully, on a practical level students should investigate the law school's placement record and bar passage rates and, through various means, determine how much student loan debt graduates accumulate during their course of study, along with forecasts about projected debt after law school during loan repayment.[58]

Moreover, a popular but controversial source of information about law schools and their alleged quality is found in the *U.S. News & World Report* (USNWR) rankings (see Table 2.3 for a sample of rankings). Although there are other sites and blogs that "rank" law schools (e.g., Above the Law, Brian Leiter's Law School Rankings, Vault, and others), empirical studies show that the USNWR annual spring publication has an effect on the decision making of both applicants and law schools.[59] In the USNWR rankings, schools are now ranked into quarter percentiles (past iterations used "tiers"). The rankings contain other information, such as tuition rates and fees, enrollment data, median UGPA and LSAT scores, and acceptance rates (but, in terms of the latter two bits of information, only for a fee). In 2017, the USNWR placed Yale, Harvard, Stanford, Columbia, and Chicago in the top spots. Notably, each has a reported tuition rate (plus fees) in excess of $56,000 per year for full-time study.

In ranking schools, the USNWR examines a weighted average of several factors: quality assessments (peer assessments and assessments by lawyers and judges), selectivity (median LSAT scores, median UGPA, and acceptance rate), placement success, bar exam passage rate, and faculty resources (expenditure per student, student–faculty ratio, and library resources). Only the top hundred to top three-quarters of the schools are included in the numerical rankings: the rest, all in the bottom quarter of ranked schools, are treated differently (alphabetically listed as "Rank Not Published"). As Table 2.3 shows, the top-rated schools value especially

Table 2.3 Law School Rankings

Rank	School	UGPA/ LSAT	Tuition and Fees	Acceptance Rate
1	Yale University	3.93/173	$58,050	9.72%
2 (tie)	Harvard University	3.86/173	$58,242	17.87%
2 (tie)	Stanford University	3.89/171	$56,274	11.25%
4 (tie)	Columbia University	3.71/172	$62,274	21.88%
4 (tie)	University of Chicago	3.90/170	$58,065	21.89%
6	New York University	3.78/169	$59,330	33.10%
7	University of Pennsylvania	3.89/169	$58,918	18.80%
8 (tie)#	University of California, Berkeley	3.78/166	$48,625* $52,576**	21.18%
8 (tie)#	University of Michigan, Ann Arbor	3.76/168	$53,112* $56,112**	27.98%
8 (tie)#	University of Virginia	3.86/168	$54,000* $57,000**	20.16%
50 (tie)#	Florida State University	3.52/158	$20,683* $40,695**	43.92%
50 (tie)#	Temple University^	3.50/160	$23,336* $36,336**	43.14%
50 (tie)	Tulane University^	3.41/161	$48,456	51.06%
50 (tie)#	University of California, Hastings^	3.50/159	$48,638* $54,638**	42.09%
50 (tie)#	University of Houston	3.54/159	$29,784* $44,044	38.29%
100 (tie)#	Indiana University, Indianapolis^	3.40/152	$25,625* $45,210**	69.72%
100 (tie)	Michigan State University^	3.46/154	$39,353	46.36%
100 (tie)#	SUNY Buffalo Law School	3.44/154	$26,997* $45,007**	51.65%
103 (tie)	Catholic University of America	3.32/153	$46,815	55.21%

Rank	School	UGPA/ LSAT	Tuition and Fees	Acceptance Rate
103 (tie)#	Florida International University^	3.61/156	$21,406* $35,650**	29.19%
103 (tie)	Stetson University^	3.28/154	$40,256	51.14%

Source: U.S. News & World Report Rankings (2017) and 2015 ABA-required disclosure reports. 50th percentile UGPA/LSAT reported.

Notes: * Resident; ** Nonresident. # Public school; all others are private. ^ Uses conditional scholarships. A total of 196 schools are ranked, so each of the first three quarters represents 49 schools. USNWR lists the bottom quarter of schools, but does not rank them.

high LSAT scores (a metric that drives law school reputation and rankings, which probably makes it the dominant factor in admissions decisions); and lower-ranked schools accept more students having weaker UGPAs and LSAT scores, a statistic that may help explain related findings by empirical studies showing that UGPAs and LSAT results are important predictors of law school success.[60]

Since their systematic introduction in 1990, the rankings have been extensively looked to as measures of law school quality by prospective students, law school administrators, law faculty, and legal practitioners. Even so, the rankings have been subjected to severe criticism, and students who review them should use an abundance of caution in interpreting what they mean or in relying on them as a basis to select their school of choice. A multitude of investigative exposés, academic studies, congressional hearings, "scamblogs," *mea culpa* admissions from law school deans, and lawsuits demonstrate that law schools have taken advantage of the ranking system in order to artificially boost rankings.[61]

To illustrate the scope of the abuse, Brian Tamanaha's *Failing Law Schools* (2012) reports that in 2011 the *New York Times*, in an exposé, disclosed that law schools were manipulating their post-JD employment data in order to create the false impression that their graduates were gainfully employed. The reality was that the legal marketplace was in the midst of a recession and the opposite was occurring—essentially, law schools were fudging how they reported the data to remain competitive and improve their reputation, a move that spiraled into other shady (and long-standing) practices that showed that (especially elite or wannabe) law schools vied to boost rankings by (1) offering "bait and switch" conditional scholarships (luring students in on a guarantee of three years of funding but then rescinding the offer when a student cannot maintain the grades to keep it due to "grading on the curve" methodologies), (2) changing their admissions formula, and (3) undertaking expensive promotional campaigns and adopting institutional strategies to inflate the school's (and faculty's) reputation, among other things. As Table 2.3 reveals, several schools in the lower ranks still use conditional scholarships in spite of the criticisms.[62]

Additionally, multiple studies have uncovered how the methodology used by the USNWR to create the rankings is deeply flawed and highly misleading. The deception, in turn, led to lawsuits by disgruntled students that sought civil damages for the harm that was caused to them by law schools that intentionally misrepresented employment data; and, in addition to deans being fired, online blogs publicized the law schools' bad behavior in a brutal and unflattering light.[63] Although some critics acknowledge that it makes sense for students to consult the rankings for a limited range of informational purposes, they argue the system that the USNWR uses to rank law schools is "unduly influential" because it "assigns arbitrary weights to incomplete measures, uses uninformed reputational surveys as proxies for quality, and forces schools to complete in an academic arms race that inflates costs." In light of these concerns, the USNWR rankings, and even alternative rankings that are readily available across the Internet such as those from Above the Law or Brian Leiter, must be assessed with a wary eye.[64]

In fact, some legal experts go further to argue that relying on conventional assessments of law schools like rankings is a recipe for failure. For Nancy Levit and Douglas O. Linder, authors of *The Happy Lawyer*, applicants too quickly fall into the trap of thinking that they are "buying a legal education." Instead, choosing a law school should be equated with "buying a peer group" within the law school community that shares the same ethical values and worldview of the applicant. Rather than pick a law school because it has high rankings or can best secure a coveted judicial clerkship, Levit and Linder recommend it is essential to visit the law schools and interact with the students, faculty, and administrators as much as possible, in and outside of classroom visits. Doing so gives needed insight as to whether the law school environment is civil, whether its faculty or alumni are empathetic to the real-life problems of clients and students and not unduly adversarial, or whether the advising or placement services collaborate with students on a one-on-one and not an impersonal basis. In positing that "[l]aw is a people profession" and that it is wise to "[s]earch for a law school where professors understand and teach the importance of social bonds," they maintain it is crucial to find a school that "seems to care about your future and can best guide you to a lifetime of happy lawyering." Thus, they assert that "[b]y far the best indicator of a good law school match" is "how well you like, respect, and trust the students who will become your peers and whether you are stimulated by them."[65]

APPLYING TO LAW SCHOOL

The decision to apply to law school should only come at the end of a preliminary but thorough investigation about the nature of the legal profession and some of the challenges in becoming a lawyer. Understanding the importance of UGPA, the LSAT, educational financing, what lawyers do, and how they are trained (considered more in depth in the next chapter) is essential knowledge that permits a full appreciation for the rewards and challenges that lie ahead. In this regard, the facts and perspective that are gathered about the legal profession before an application is submitted are the foundation for confidently developing a short list of desirable law schools that fit the applicant's qualifications and expectations.

Once the decision is made to apply, the next step is to prepare an application that the law school admissions committee will assess favorably in comparison to the hundreds of others they will be reviewing in the admissions cycle for the new academic year. In submitting applications, it is always worth bearing in mind that getting into law school is a competitive and time-consuming process. Accordingly, there is no guarantee of acceptance, but if the necessary preparation is done beforehand, the chances for admission success improve greatly. In this section, the logistics for applying to law school are discussed along with some of the special issues that may arise in preparing the application and having to respond to the application if circumstances dictate. Thereafter, the discussion turns to identifying some of the important elements in making a final decision once the admission letters, or denials or wait list notices, start to arrive.

Preparing the Law School Application

Once a working list of law schools has been compiled, the next step is to begin the application process. Students navigating through its logistics should routinely consult with the prelaw advising and career services that are offered through their undergraduate institutions if questions arise or additional guidance is necessary; or, alternatively, LSAC resources and several commercial self-help guides are readily available online or in print for additional consultation.[66] Since every school has its own admission process, it is imperative to become familiar with each school's requirements early on. For context and review, the general steps and timeline for initiating and completing the law school application are outlined in Table 2.4.

Table 2.4 Law School Application Process

Timeline	Action Required
Freshman/ Sophomore Years	• Make decisions about prelaw coursework and academic preparation • Perform well academically (high UGPA) • Consult with prelaw adviser and career services • Consult informally with attorneys/judges or alumni who work in law • Read recommended prelaw and law career readings • Join prelaw club and/or other extracurricular activities • After thorough self-assessment, determine if law study or career is still of interest and commit to further preparation or not • Become familiar with LSAC, LSAT, and CAS requirements (and fees) and law school application process • Begin to examine law schools online and in person • Understand cost and educational financing issues • Contact law school admissions personnel and begin to visit schools of interest, including faculty and classroom visits

(Continued)

Table 2.4   (Continued)

Timeline	Action Required
Junior Year	• Begin LSAT preparation (200+ hours required) • Create short list of law schools of interest (5–7 ideally) • Attend LSAC Law Forums • Create LSAC account online • Prepare résumé and update continuously • Begin to write personal statement and/or other supplemental essays • Register for June (or September) LSAT and CAS online • Take June (or September) LSAT
Senior Year	• Arrange for official transcripts to be sent • Request letters of recommendation from professors and other employment contacts or professionals (no later than spring semester) • Finish and compile required documentation, including addendum (if necessary to explain weaker LSAT score and/or UPGA), supplemental essays (only to select schools of high interest), and dean certification (if required) • Complete and submit law school applications (5 or fewer law schools, ideally, by October for next fall admission) • Explore logistics and do financial cost assessment of schools that offer admission • Make final decision

Source: Law School Admission Council, "Applying to Law School," accessed August 9, 2016, from http://lsac.org/jd/applying-to-law-school/overview.

Although several items of the action plan listed in Table 2.4 transpire in the first two years of undergraduate education, the application process begins in earnest in the third, or junior, year of study. In the junior year, students must direct their primary efforts at preparing for, and taking, the LSAT (which, ideally in June or by the latest September, can be taken for the first time, or as a repeat test if needed, in order to submit an application by next fall); but, other steps, such as beginning the process of writing a personal statement (which explains the personal reasons, and special qualities, for wanting to attend law school) and a résumé or other essays (that should be tailored for law school admission committee review), must be initiated as well. Further, the groundwork for requesting two to three letters of recommendation should already be established by the end of the junior year; that is, before actually requesting the letters in the senior year, students should have already built the foundation for getting written testimonials from professionals (professors, employers, or community leaders) who can speak confidently and knowingly about an applicant's ability to undertake the rigors of graduate school law school study. In selecting letter writers, applicants must choose wisely and only ask trusted persons with whom a classroom, work, or community-based relationship has been solidly established, preferably over time. Applicants must also give recommenders sufficient lead time and information to write the references. In order to ease the task and orient the writing, students should supply busy and time-constrained letter writers with a written but brief synopsis of any relevant information that will assist them, such as grade summaries, law school aspirations and motivations, unusual personal circumstances, extraordinary accomplishments or extracurricular activities, drafts of résumés and personal statements, and applicable deadlines and logistics.[67]

Achieving early success in the LSAT in the junior year has the advantage of allowing students to turn their complete attention to the time-consuming process of compiling the extensive documentation that must accompany law school applications. Depending on the school requirements and in accordance with the discretionary choices made by applicants to bolster their files, in addition to forwarding official transcripts and securing letters of recommendation, many applicants prepare personal statements, résumés, supplemental essays, addenda, and a dean's certification (supplying academic information about attendance, majors, minors, UGPA, and the like). Moreover, most applications require disclosure of issues and facts that raise character and fitness issues, such as past academic misconduct or criminal activities, in their records and personal backgrounds. For most applicants, the CAS, which most ABA-approved law schools require students to use, streamlines the application process by collecting and distributing LSAT scores and writing samples, academic transcripts, an admission index (a formula combining an LSAT score and UGPA into an index number, if required by the school), letters of recommendation, and miscellaneous relevant information.[68]

Of the remaining documents, the personal statement is of utmost importance. Generally, personal statements are the vehicle to let applicants explain their personal story and qualifications for undertaking law study. In many respects, they are easy to write if applicants invest the time to understand fully the reasons why they want to be a lawyer—something that should result after undergoing a thorough self-assessment and an investigation of legal profession and law training in the early years of undergraduate study (see Table 2.4). For example, if a school boasts a special program or course of study, applicants will already know how to customize their generic version of the personal statement and use it to get noticed by the admission committee and gain an edge on the competition. Still, even applicants who have done their initial homework may still underestimate the time and effort that goes into writing an effective personal statement. The personal statement is a critical element of law school applications because admissions committees, which read thousands of applications in any given admissions cycle, will quickly disregard statements (and applications, especially if on the bubble) from applicants that are poorly written and do not help distinguish the candidate from others who are vying for coveted seats in a competitive application process.[69]

While many undergraduate institutions and commercial "how to" books may render advice on how to write personal statements, as a rule of thumb students ought to strive for economy (no more than two pages) and originality in writing essays that immediately grab the committee's attention, preferably in the first sentence. This can be done by constructing a personal profile that is interesting and goes beyond a rote recitation of the raw numbers (i.e., UGPA and LSAT score). By anecdote or otherwise, personal statements should give special insight about an applicant's life, intellect, motivation, maturity, and commitment to law study. A common mistake is to convey how law school will benefit an applicant's life by potentially reaping lucrative employment, personal fame, or financial rewards and the like. Rather, committees are more interested in learning how an applicant's personal skill set and unique experiences will make an enduring contribution to the law school community and the legal profession as a whole. Explanations about weaknesses in the file, such as a weak LSAT score or a less-than-stellar UGPA, should be reserved for the addendum, which applicants add to accentuate application strengths that are not discussed in the personal statements or elsewhere. As with any important writing that will be judged by others, applicants must take great care in preparing it with an outline, multiple drafts, extensive proofreading, and a revision process that enables trusted peers, academicians, and career professionals (with undergraduate institutions) to review and offer grammar, style, or substantive content suggestions.[70]

The same attention to time and detail must be given to completing character and fitness statements (or arranging dean's certifications, if required, that supply academic standing information, including disciplinary or misconduct issues), résumés, addenda, or supplemental essays. All of these elements are designed to increase the chances for favorable admission outcomes in a highly competitive application process. In satisfying character and fitness requirements, applicants must fully disclose all pertinent information lest the committee discover, after the fact, that there is an ethical failing or omission that suggests the candidate is not being up front, transparent, and candid about such misfeasance. For résumés, committees expect to receive polished and professionally formatted writings that are grammatically sound and descriptive of key information, including educational background, work history, volunteerism, travel or military experience, and research interests, among others. Any work or volunteer experience in the legal field should be emphasized in a separate section of the résumé. Addenda and other supplemental essays, on the other hand, are typically optional but selectively target schools of great interest. They serve a number of significant purposes: they may explain UGPA or LSAT weaknesses, or past misconduct; unusual or extenuating circumstances; barriers that have been overcome; interests in a specific school or program; or how an applicant's past experiences have enhanced public service or will contribute to the diversity and quality of the incoming law school class and the profession as a whole.

In addition to written documentation, some, but not all, law schools permit a personal interview as part of the application process (either by invitation, by request, or informally). While some schools disallow or discourage interviews (due to high volume and lack of resources), it is not uncommon for applicants to take the initiative to meet with admissions staff, faculty members, or law school alumni on an informal basis during a school visit or perhaps an extended telephone conversation. As with all parts of the application process, informal interviewing must only occur after applicants have thoroughly prepared for it. Interviewing gives candidates an excellent opportunity to explain the nuances of the underlying application while being exposed to the school's strengths and weaknesses on a firsthand basis. Moreover, what the school learns about the applicant during informal interviewing is often shared with the admissions committee or placed in the applicant's file for further evaluation. As a result, as one law school dean puts it, interviewing "is well worth the reward, provided prospective students are willing to take the time to prepare."[71]

Law school admission committees evaluate applications on a rolling basis, a process that populates the incoming class by making admission decisions on a continuous basis until all the available seats are filled. The system, therefore, rewards applicants who submit their applications well ahead of the application deadline. While schools vary in establishing their deadlines, a common approach is to begin to evaluate applications in the mid-summer to fall time period of the calendar year before the anticipated enrollment date, which typically occurs in the fall semester. As well, some schools offer early decision and early admission options, which accelerates the time frame for applying by several months (typically, by early winter). Early admissions ordinarily advantage two types of applicants: those who know that a specific school is a first choice and, perhaps, those with UGPA and LSAT scores that are outside of the school's normal threshold requirements ("stretch schools" that might be more receptive to applications received early on in the admissions process). While early admission applicants may receive the cost (and reduction of anxiety) benefit of receiving a favorable decision early in the admissions cycle, schools may require that all other law school applications be withdrawn upon acceptance; and any eligibility for deferring admissions to a later date will be forfeited. Therefore, exercising early admission options should be done with extreme care since they exact a commitment that not only dramatically reduces law school choices, but also binds students to attend even though they might not yet be fully aware of their financial aid packages (including scholarships or tuition discounts) on the date they are required to tender a nonrefundable seat deposit.[72]

CONCLUSION

After reviewing applications, the admissions committee will generally deliver the news that an applicant has been accepted, rejected, or put on a wait list (a form of conditional admission that admits students only when another applicant has been accepted but opts not to attend). Although many schools permit appeals from rejections, the practice is frowned upon unless there is a strong indication that something in the file significantly changed and improved the application from the time of original submission. On the other hand, admissions committees are more receptive to additional input coming from wait-listed students, so long as the communications are not excessive and off-putting. Many law school admission committees, therefore, might look favorably upon a wait-listed student who writes a short letter or note of continuing interest, especially if applicants can point to some improvement in LSAT scores (that might have been earned after original submission) or some other indicia that strengthen admission chances, like the publication of a master's thesis or other accomplishments.[73]

As alluded to earlier, it should be borne in mind that, after acceptance, certain highly qualified students may receive competing offers to attend from different law schools, and many schools are willing to negotiate the terms of merit-based financial aid or scholarships. Under such circumstances, the choice to attend a specific school should only be made after doing extensive research and performing a careful evaluation of what is being proposed in light of student financial needs, personal circumstances, or career goals. A critical element in such negotiations, for example, is determining if the school is conditioning its offer of aid (by grade performance or other criteria), or if the money will not be withdrawn during a student's course of study. Whether a law school offers conditional scholarships is discovered from making inquiries to law schools, or by exploring the ABA's Standard 509 Information Reports and other online sources. Regardless, for accepted students, the preparation that went into applying will have to be redirected with a new energy and vigor to making the transition from undergraduate to graduate law study, a topic taken up in the next chapter.

SELECTED READINGS

Glendon, Mary Ann. *A Nation under Lawyers: How the Crisis in the Legal Profession Is Transforming American Society*. Cambridge, Mass.: Harvard University Press, 1996.

Ivey, Anna. *The Ivey Guide to Law School Admissions: Straight Advice on Essays, Resumes, Interviews, and More*. Orlando, Fla.: Harcourt, 2005.

Johnson, Creola. *Is a Law Degree Still Worth the Price? It Depends on What the Law School Has to Offer You*. Durham, N.C.: Carolina Academic Press, 2014.

Levine, Anne K. *The Law School Admission Game: Play like an Expert*. Santa Barbara, Calif.: Abraham, 2013.

Montauk, Richard. *How to Get into the Top Law Schools*, 5th ed. New York, N.Y.: Prentice Hall, 2011.

Schneider, Deborah, and Gary Belsky. *Should You Really Be a Lawyer? The 2013 Guide to Smart Career Choices before, during, and after Law School*, 2nd ed. Seattle, WA: LawyerAvenue Press, 2013.

Stake, Jeffrey Evans, and Michael Alexeev, "Who Responds to *U.S. News & World Report*'s Law School Rankings?," *Journal of Empirical Legal Studies* 12 (2015): 421–480.

WEB LINKS

American Bar Association (www.americanbar.org)
Law School Admission Council (www.lsac.org)
Law School Transparency (www.lawschooltransparency.com)

ENDNOTES

1. Mary Ann Glendon, *A Nation under Lawyers: How the Crisis in the Legal Profession Is Transforming American Society* (Cambridge, Mass.: Harvard University Press, 1996). See also Sheldon Krantz, *The Legal Profession: What Is Wrong and How to Fix It* (New Providence, N.J.: LexisNexis, 2014), 11; American Bar Association, "ABA National Lawyer Population Survey Historical Trend in Total National Lawyer Population 1878–2016," accessed May 4, 2016, from www.americanbar.org/content/dam/aba/administrative/market_research/total-national-lawyer-population-1878-2016.authcheckdam.pdf; U.S. Census Bureau, "Number of Firms, Number of Establishments, Employment, Annual Payroll, and Receipts by Employment Size of the Enterprise for the United States, All Industries—2002," available from www.census.gov (last retrieved May 15, 2014); Philip G. Schrag, "MOOCS and Legal Education: Valuable Innovation or Looming Disaster?,"

Villanova Law Review 59 (2014): 83–134. See also Mansfield J. Park, "The Best Online Law Schools: JD and LLM Programs," *Above the Law* (May 2, 2013), accessed May 4, 2016, from http://abovethelaw.com/career-files/the-best-online-law-schools-jd-and-llm-programs/; MarketLine, "Legal Services in the United States (October 2012, Reference Code: 0072–0423)," available at www.marketline.com (last retrieved May 12, 2014).

2. Robert L. Nelson and Gabriele Plickert, "Introduction," in *After the JD III: Third Results from a National Study of Legal Careers*, ed. Gabriele Plickert (Chicago, Ill.: American Bar Foundation; Dallas, Texas: NALP Foundation for Law Career Research and Education, 2014), 14.

3. Sheldon Krantz, *The Legal Profession: What Is Wrong and How to Fix It* (New Providence, N.J.: LexisNexis, 2014), 19. Each jurisdiction's bar requirements are found in National Conference of Bar Examiners and American Bar Association Section of Legal Education and Admissions to the Bar, *Comprehensive Guide to Bar Admission Requirements: 2016*, accessed July 25, 2016, from www.ncbex.org/pubs/bar-admis sions-guide/2016/index.html#p=4. See also Sustainable Economics Law Center, "Like Lincoln: Becoming a Lawyer without Going to Law School (State-by-State Guide to Apprenticeships)," accessed on July 25, 2016, from http://likelincoln.org/state-by-state-guide-to-apprenticeships/; Board of Bar Examiners, "Admission to the Practice of Law in Wisconsin: Diploma Privilege 2017," accessed February 14, 2017, from www.wicourts .gov/services/attorney/bardiploma.htm.

4. National Association for Law Placement Inc., "Detailed Analysis of JD Advantage Jobs," accessed August 1, 2016, from www.nalp.org/jd_advantage_jobs_detail_may2013. The quotation earlier in the paragraph is from Nancy Levit and Douglas O. Linder, *The Happy Lawyer: Making a Good Life in the Law* (New York, N.Y.: Oxford University Press, 2010), 115. See also Douglas O. Linder and Nancy Levit, *The Good Lawyer: Seeking Quality in the Practice of Law* (New York, N.Y.: Oxford University Press, 2014), 288–289.

5. John Monahan and Jeffrey Swanson, "Lawyers at Mid-career: A 20-Year Longitudinal Study of Job and Life Satisfaction," *Journal of Empirical Legal Studies* 6 (2009): 451–483.

6. Rebecca Sandefur and Robert L. Nelson, "Mobility and Turnover," in *After the JD III: Third Results from a National Study of Legal Careers*, ed. Gabriele Plickert (Chicago, Ill.: American Bar Foundation; Dallas, Texas: NALP Foundation for Law Career Research and Education, 2014), 58–61. The definition and relevance of so-called JD Advantage jobs are subject to ongoing controversy; see Creola Johnson, *Is a Law Degree Still Worth the Price? It Depends on What the Law School Has to Offer You* (Durham, N.C.: Carolina Academic Press, 2014), 81–85.

7. The rate of law school graduation typically fluctuates from year to year but stays within the same 40,000–46,000 range. In 2014, there were 43,832 graduates; in 2013, 46,364; and in 2012, 43,979. Between 2008 and 2012, on average 44,564 students graduated from law school. Law school graduation data, along with matriculation, enrollment, and attrition rates, are found in American Bar Association, "Statistics," accessed December 30, 2016, from www.americanbar.org/groups/legal_education/resources/statistics.html; and American Bar Association, "2016 Standard 509 Information Report Data Overview," accessed December 30, 2016, from www.americanbar.org/content/dam/aba/administra tive/legal_education_and_admissions_to_the_bar/statistics/2016_standard_509_data_ overview.authcheckdam.pdf.

8. Thomas W. Lyons, "Legal Education: Learning What Lawyers Need," in *The Relevant Lawyer: Reimagining the Future of the Legal Profession*, ed. Paul A. Haskins (Chicago, Ill.: American Bar Association, 2015), 226.

9. American Bar Association, "ABA National Lawyer Population Survey 10-Year Trend in Lawyer Population by State, Year 2016," accessed May 4, 2016, from www.americanbar .org/content/dam/aba/administrative/market_research/national-lawyer-population-by-state-2006-2016.authcheckdam.pdf.

10. Krantz, *Legal Profession*, 14. See also National Association for Law Placement, "Women and Minorities at Law Firms by Race and Ethnicity—New Findings for 2015 (Table 1)," accessed May 4, 2016, from www.nalp.org/0116research; National Association for Law Placement, "LGBT Representation among Lawyers in 2015 (Table 1)," accessed May 4, 2016, from www.nalp.org/1215research; National Association for Law Placement, "Still Relatively Few Openly GLBT or Disabled Lawyers Reported (Table 1)," accessed May 4, 2016, from www.nalp.org/2005decfewopenlyglbtdisabled; American Bar Association, Commission on Women in the Profession, "A Current Glance at Women in the Law (May 2016)," accessed May 4, 2016, from www.americanbar.org/content/dam/aba/marketing/women/current_glance_statistics_may2016.authcheckdam.pdf; American Bar Association, Commission on Mental and Physical Disability Law, "ABA Disability Statistics Report (2011)," accessed May 4, 2016, from www.americanbar.org/content/dam/aba/uncategorized/2011/20110314_aba_disability_statistics_report.authcheckdam.pdf.

11. National Association of Law Placement, "Class of 2015 National Summary Report," accessed August 23, 2016, from www.nalp.org/uploads/NatlSummaryClassof2015.pdf.

12. Ronit Dinovitzer, "Practice Setting," in *After the JD III: Third Results from a National Study of Legal Careers*, ed. Gabriele Plickert (Chicago, Ill.: American Bar Foundation; Dallas, Texas: NALP Foundation for Law Career Research and Education, 2014), 26.

13. Deborah L. Rhode, *The Trouble with Lawyers* (New York, N.Y.: Oxford University Press, 2015), 10. See also Krantz, *Legal Profession*, 31; National Association of Law Placement, "Class of 2015 National Summary Report"; and National Association of Law Placement, "Employment for the Class of 2015—Selected Findings," accessed December 30, 2016, from www.nalp.org/uploads/Membership/EmploymentfortheClassof2015SelectedFindings.pdf (declaring that in respect to the 2015 class, "the entry-level legal market" is "remarkably flat by almost every measure").

14. Law School Admission Council and American Bar Association Section of Legal Education and Admissions to the Bar, *ABA-LSAC Official Guide to ABA-Approved Law Schools (2013 Edition)* (Newtown, Pa.: Law School Admission Council, 2012), 1–3. See also Krantz, *Legal Profession*, 32. On the issue of professional stratification and recent trends, see Herbert M. Kritzer, *Lawyers at Work* (New Orleans, La.: Quid Pro Books, 2015), 271–273; and Richard Sander and Jane Bambauer, "The Secret of My Success: How Status, Eliteness, and School Performance Shape Legal Careers," *Journal of Empirical Legal Studies* 9 (2012): 893, 899. Seminal studies include John Heinz and Edward O. Laumann, *Chicago Lawyers: The Social Structure of the Bar* (New York, N.Y.: Russell Sage Foundation, 1982); John P. Heinz, Robert L. Nelson, and Edward O. Laumann, "The Scale of Justice: Observations on the Transformation of Urban Law Practice," *Annual Review of Sociology* 27 (2001): 337–362; and John P. Heinz et al., *Urban Lawyers: The New Social Structure of the Bar* (Chicago, Ill.: University of Chicago Press, 2005).

15. Levit and Linder, *Happy Lawyer*, 117–118. The quoted material is from Sander and Bambauer, "Secret of My Success," 893–930.

16. The quotation is from Krantz, *Legal Profession*, 51. See also Heinz et al., *Urban Lawyers*.

17. Ronit Dinovitzer, "The Financial Rewards of Elite Status in the Legal Profession," *Law and Social Inquiry* 36 (2011): 971, 989.

18. Krantz, *Legal Profession*, 59. See also National Association for Legal Career Professionals, "Prelaw—What Do Lawyers Do?," accessed May 17, 2016, from www.nalp.org/what_do_lawyers_do?s=general%20counsel.

19. Stephen M. Sheppard, "The American Legal Profession in the Twenty-first Century," *American Journal of Comparative Law* 62 (2014): 241, 270.

20. National Association of Law Placement, "Class of 2015 National Summary Report." See also National Association of Law Placement, "How Much Do Law Firms Pay Associates? A Look Back at 20 Years of Findings from the NALP Associate Salary

Survey," accessed September 14, 2016, from www.nalp.org/1014research; and National Association of Law Placement, "Jobs & JDs: Employment for the Class of 2015—Selected Findings," accessed September 14, 2016, from www.nalp.org/uploads/Membership/EmploymentfortheClassof2015SelectedFindings.pdf.

21. The LST Score Reports are accessible from Law School Transparency, "Using the Score Reports," accessed December 30, 2016, from www.lstreports.com/guides/.

22. National Association of Law Placement, "Class of 2014 Bimodal Salary Curve," accessed December 30, 2016, from www.nalp.org/class_of_2014_salary_curve.

23. Benjamin H. Barton, *Glass Half Full: The Decline and Rebirth of the Legal Profession* (New York, N.Y.: Oxford University Press, 2015), 45. The NALP data in historical perspective are found in Judith N. Collins, "Salaries for New Lawyers: An Update on Where We Are and How We Got Here," accessed December 30, 2016, from www.nalp.org/uploads/0812Research.pdf.

24. Elizabeth Olson, "Law Firm Salaries Jump for the First Time in Nearly a Decade," *New York Times* (June 6, 2016), accessed August 3, 2016, from www.nytimes.com/2016/06/07/business/dealbook/law-firm-salaries-jump-for-the-first-time-in-nearly-a-decade.html?_r=0.

25. National Association for Law Placement, "Class of 2015 National Summary Report"; National Association for Law Placement, "Jobs & JDs."

26. Krantz, *Legal Profession*, 31 (figures based on 2010 Bureau of Labor Statistics data).

27. American Bar Association, "Data from the 2013 Annual Questionnaire: ABA Approved Law School Tuition History Data," accessed May 18, 2016, from www.americanbar.org/groups/legal_education/resources/statistics.html.

28. American Bar Association, "Average Living and Book Expenses for Single Students Living on Campus, 1990–2012," accessed May 18, 2016, from www.americanbar.org/content/dam/aba/administrative/legal_education_and_admissions_to_the_bar/statistics/average_living_book_expenses.authcheckdam.pdf.

29. The figures stated here are for 2011–2012 and 2012–2013, though the ABA altered the way it reported debt levels after the first period. In 2011–2012, the data were based on the question, "The average amount borrowed in law school by J.D. graduates who borrowed at least one education loan in law school," which yielded an average debt of $84,600 for public law schools and $122,258 for private ones. Beginning in 2012–2013, the question was, "The average amount borrowed in law school by J.D. students who borrowed at least one education loan in any amount in the previous academic year," which yielded an average debt level of $32,289 (public) and $44,094 (private). American Bar Association, "From 2013 Questionnaire—ABA Approved Average Amount Borrowed: Fall 2013," accessed May 18, 2016, from www.americanbar.org/content/dam/aba/administrative/legal_education_and_admissions_to_the_bar/statistics/2013_fall_avg_amnt_brwd.xls.

30. Law School Transparency, "Cost of Attendance," accessed December 31, 2016, from www.lstreports.com/guides/Cost-of-Attendance/.

31. Rebecca Sandefur, Bryant G. Garth, and Joyce Sterling, "Financing Legal Education: The View Twelve Years out of Law School," in *After the JD III: Third Results from a National Study of Legal Careers*, ed. Gabriele Plickert (Chicago, Ill.: American Bar Foundation; Dallas, Texas: NALP Foundation for Law Career Research and Education, 2014), 80–84.

32. The conditional scholarship practice, and which law schools engage in it (and with what outcomes in terms of retention rates), is explained in Law School Transparency, "Conditional Scholarships," accessed December 31, 2016, from www.lawschooltransparency.com/reform/projects/Conditional-Scholarships/. For criticisms, see Debra Cassens Weiss, "Which Law Schools Were Most Likely to Yank Merit-based Scholarships?," *ABA Journal* (July 8, 2013), accessed December 31, 2016, from www.abajournal.com/news/article/which_law_schools_were_most_likely_to_yank_merit-based_scholarships/. Standard 509 Information Reports are found on ABA-accredited law school websites.

33. Law School Transparency, "Student Loans," accessed December 31, 2016, from www .lstreports.com/guides/Student-Loans/. For loan payment and forgiveness options, see U.S. Department of Education, "Federal Student Aid," accessed December 31, 2016, from https://studentaid.ed.gov/sa/types/loans/subsidized-unsubsidized; and American Bar Association, "Student Loan Repayment and Forgiveness," accessed May 18, 2016, from www.americanbar.org/groups/legal_education/resources/student_loan_repayment_ and_forgiveness.html.

34. Law professor Benjamin Barton cites empirical studies showing that law graduates must make roughly $65,000 annually to make their student loan payments, but more than 40 percent do not start at law jobs that pay that much. Barton, *Glass Half Full*, 148.

35. Brian Z. Tamanaha, *Failing Law Schools* (Chicago, Ill.: University of Chicago Press, 2012), 197.

36. Law School Admission Council, "Choosing a Law School: How to Evaluate Law Schools," accessed August 3, 2016, from http://lsac.org/jd/choosing-a-law-school/evaluating-law-schools. See also Sander and Bambauer, "Secret of My Success," 893, 901 (reporting that data from a national study of law school performance show that first-year students are overly optimistic about the grades they receive, before their first set of exams).

37. American Bar Association Section of Legal Education and Admissions to the Bar, "Pre-law," accessed May 16, 2016, from www.americanbar.org/groups/legal_education/ resources/pre_law.html; Law School Admission Council, "Thinking about Law School: Preparing for Law School," accessed May 16, 2016, from www.lsac.org/jd/thinking-about-law-school/preparing-for-law-school.

38. Derek Muller, "Which Undergraduate Majors Are the Best Law Students?," accessed August 5, 2016, from http://excessofdemocracy.com/blog/2015/4/which-undergraduate-majors-are-the-best-law-students-featuring-interactive-visualizations; Derek Muller, "LSAT Scores and GPAs of Law School Matriculants, Sorted by Undergraduate Major, 2013–2014," accessed August 5, 2016, from http://excessofdemocracy.com/ blog/2015/5/lsat-scores-and-gpas-of-law-school-matriculants-sorted-by-undergraduate-major-2013-2014; Alexia Brunet Marks and Scott A. Moss, "What Predicts Law Student Success? A Longitudinal Study Correlating Law Student Applicant Data and Law School Outcomes," *Journal of Empirical Legal Studies* 13 (2016): 205–265. See also American Bar Association, "Pre-law"; and Krantz, *Legal Profession*, 19.

39. For a discussion of such programs, see Elie Mystal, "Are '3+3' Programs a Good Idea?," accessed December 31, 2016, from http://abovethelaw.com/2013/11/are-3-3-programs-a-good-idea/.

40. Law School Admission Council, "Roles and Responsibilities of Pre-law Advisors," accessed May 19, 2016, from www.lsac.org/docs/default-source/prelaw/prelaw_roles-and-responsibilities.pdf?sfvrsn=2.

41. Law School Admission Council and American Bar Association Section of Legal Education and Admissions to the Bar, *ABA-LSAC Official Guide to ABA-Approved Law Schools (2013 Edition)*, 1.

42. American Bar Association, "Pre-law."

43. Sarah Valentine, "Flourish or Founder: The New Regulatory Regime in Legal Education," *Journal of Law and Education* 44 (2015): 473, 484–485. See also Krantz, *Legal Profession*, 24–25.

44. A comprehensive list of prelaw books that supply information about law school, jurisprudence, legal biographies, and the legal profession is found in Law School Admission Council, "Resources for the Prelaw Candidate," accessed May 19, 2016, from www.lsac .org/docs/default-source/jd-docs/resources-for-prelaw-candidate.pdf.

45. Ann Perry, "Interpreting the Numbers: The Importance of LSAT and UGPA in an Admission Decision," in *Getting into Law School: A Guide for Pre-law Students*, accessed May 19, 2016, from www.admissionsdean.com/downloads/GettingIntoLaw SchoolGuide.pdf.

46. Law School Admission Council and American Bar Association Section of Legal Education and Admissions to the Bar, *ABA-LSAC Official Guide to ABA-Approved Law Schools (2013 Edition)*, 9.

47. The content and logistics of taking the examination are detailed at Law School Admission Council, "Law School Admission Test," accessed August 6, 2016, from http://lsac.org/jd/lsat/about-the-lsat. See also Dave Killoran, "A Brief Overview of the LSAT," in *Getting into Law School: A Guide for Pre-law Students*, accessed May 19, 2016, from www.admissionsdean.com/downloads/GettingIntoLawSchoolGuide.pdf, 3.

48. Law School Admission Council, "Law School Admission Test: Frequently Asked Questions," accessed August 6, 2016, from http://lsac.org/jd/help/faqs-lsat.

49. Law School Admission Council, "Law School Admission Test: Fee Waivers for the LSAT & Credential Assembly Service (CAS)," accessed August 6, 2016, from www.lsac.org/jd/lsat/fee-waivers; Law School Admission Council, "Law School Admission Test: LSAT Dates & Deadlines," accessed February 15, 2017, from www.lsac.org/jd/lsat/test-dates-deadlines; and Law School Admission Council, "Law School Admission Test: Frequently Asked Questions."

50. The LSAC declares that data show that repeat test takers often raise their scores slightly, but there is always a chance that they may not. Law School Admission Council, "Law School Admission Test: Frequently Asked Questions." See also Marks and Moss, "What Predicts Law Student Success?" (finding that LSAT predicts more weakly, and UGPA predicts more powerfully, than commonly assumed; and that a high LSAT/low UGPA combination predicts worse than a high UGPA/low LSAT combination). The quoted portion of the paragraph is from an associate dean for admissions and financial aid from the University of Chicago Law School, in Ann Perry, "Interpreting the Numbers: The Importance of LSAT and UGPA in an Admission Decision," in *Getting into Law School: A Guide for Pre-law Students*, accessed May 19, 2016, from www.admissionsdean.com/downloads/GettingIntoLawSchoolGuide.pdf, 5.

51. See, e.g., Kaplan, "LSAT Prep Options," accessed May 19, 2016, from www.kaptest.com/lsat/lsat-prep-course/course-options; PowerScore, "LSAT Prep Courses," accessed May 19, 2016, from www.powerscore.com/lsat/courses.cfm; *The Princeton Review*, "Select LSAT Prep Course," accessed May 19, 2016, from www.princetonreview.com/law/lsat-test-prep. See, generally, Killoran, "A Brief Overview of the LSAT"; Law School Admission Council, "Law School Admission Test: Preparing for the LSAT," accessed August 6, 2016, from www.lsac.org/jd/lsat/preparing-for-the-lsat; and Law School Admission Council, "Law School Admission Test: Frequently Asked Questions."

52. Law School Admission Council, "Choosing a Law School: How to Evaluate Law Schools." See also Law School Admission Council, "Law School Admission Test: Frequently Asked Questions."

53. Levit and Linder, *Happy Lawyer*, 115.

54. Law School Admission Council, "2017 LSAC Law School Forums," accessed February 15, 2017, from http://lsac.org/lawschoolforums/.

55. Lyons, "Legal Education," 222–223.

56. Law School Admission Council, "About LSAC," accessed August 1, 2016, from www.lsac.org/aboutlsac/about-lsac. See also Law School Admission Council, "UGPA and LSAT Score Search," accessed August 1, 2016, from https://officialguide.lsac.org/Release/UGPALSAT/UGPALSAT.aspx; Law School Admission Council, "2017 LSAC Law School Forums."

57. Law School Admission Council, "Choosing a Law School: Law School Links," accessed May 19, 2016, from www.lsac.org/jd/choosing-a-law-school/law-school-links.

58. Helpful resources on these issues are available from the law schools themselves or online sites such as Law School Transparency. See Law School Transparency, "Welcome to Law School Transparency," accessed February 23, 2017, from www.lawschooltransparency.com. See also Law School Admission Council, "Choosing a Law School: How to Evaluate Law Schools." The ABA imposed the requirement to disclose by revising

Standard 509 in 2013. American Bar Association Section of Legal Education and Admissions to the Bar, "Memorandum (August 2013)," accessed August 1, 2016, from www.americanbar.org/content/dam/aba/administrative/legal_education_and_admissions_to_the_bar/governancedocuments/2013_standard_509_memo.authcheckdam.pdf.

59. Jeffrey Evans Stake and Michael Alexeev, "Who Responds to *U.S. News & World Report*'s Law School Rankings?," *Journal of Empirical Legal Studies* 12 (2015): 421–480. See also *U.S. News & World Report*, "Best Law Schools," accessed December 31, 2016, from http://grad-schools.usnews.rankingsandreviews.com/best-graduate-schools/top-law-schools/law-rankings?int=a1d108; Above the Law, "Law School Rankings," accessed December 31, 2016, from http://abovethelaw.com/careers/2016-law-school-rankings/; Brian Leiter, "Brian Leiter's Law School Rankings," accessed December 31, 2016, from www.leiterrankings.com/new/index.shtml; and Vault, "Best Law Schools," accessed December 31, 2016, from www.vault.com/school-rankings/best-law-schools/.

60. See, e.g., Marks and Moss, "What Predicts Law Student Success?," 205–265, 211. See also Robert Morse, "Methodology: 2017 Best Law Schools Rankings," *U.S. News & World Report*, accessed December 31, 2016, from www.usnews.com/education/best-graduate-schools/articles/law-schools-methodology?page=3.

61. Tamanaha, *Failing Law Schools*, 71–84.

62. Ibid., 71–72, 74–78. See also David Segal, "Is Law School a Losing Game?" *New York Times* (January 8, 2011); and David Segal, "Law Students Lose the Grant Game as Schools Win," *New York Times* (April 30, 2011).

63. Barton, *Glass Half Full*, 156–159; Tamanaha, *Failing Law Schools*, 75–80. See also Brian Leiter, "The *U.S. News* Law School Rankings: A Guide for the Perplexed," *Brian Leiter's Law School Rankings* (May 2003), accessed May 20, 2016, from www.leiterrankings.com/usnews/guide.shtml.

64. Above the Law, "Top 50 Law Schools 2015," accessed May 20, 2016, from http://abovethelaw.com/careers/2015-law-school-rankings/; Brian Leiter, "Newest Rankings," *Brien Leiter's Law School Rankings*, accessed May 20, 2016, from www.leiterrankings.com/new/index.shtml. The quoted material is found in Rhode, *Trouble with Lawyers*, 123.

65. Levit and Linder, *Happy Lawyer*, 116–123.

66. Anne K. Levine, *The Law School Admission Game: Play Like an Expert* (Santa Barbara, Calif.: Abraham, 2013); Deborah Schneider and Gary Belsky, *Should You Really Be a Lawyer? The 2013 Guide to Smart Career Choices before, during, and after Law School*, 2nd ed. (Seattle, Wash.: LawyerAvenue Press, 2013); Richard Montauk, *How to Get into the Top Law Schools*, 5th ed. (New York, N.Y.: Prentice Hall, 2011); Anna Ivey, *The Ivey Guide to Law School Admissions: Straight Advice on Essays, Resumes, Interviews, and More* (Orlando, Fla.: Harcourt, 2005).

67. See Renee Post and Sarah Zearfoss, "Letters of Recommendation," in *Getting into Law School: A Guide for Pre-law Students*, accessed May 19, 2016, from www.admissionsdean.com/downloads/GettingIntoLawSchoolGuide.pdf, 3.

68. Law School Admission Council, "Applying to Law School: Law School Reports," accessed August 9, 2016, from http://lsac.org/jd/applying-to-law-school/cas/law-school-reports.

69. See Thomas Lambert, "Writing a Winning Personal Statement," in *Getting into Law School: A Guide for Pre-Law Students*, accessed May 19, 2016, from www.admissionsdean.com/downloads/GettingIntoLawSchoolGuide.pdf, 6. See, generally, Montauk, *How to Get into the Top Law Schools*, 263–320.

70. Lambert, "Writing a Winning Personal Statement," 6; Montauk, *How to Get into the Top Law Schools*, 263–267, 301–320. See, generally, Eric Owens, *Law School Essays That Made a Difference*, 6th ed. (Natick, Mass.: Princeton Review, 2014).

71. Monica Ingram, "The Law School Admissions Interview," in *Getting into Law School: A Guide for Pre-law Students*, accessed May 19, 2016, from www.admissionsdean.com/downloads/GettingIntoLawSchoolGuide.pdf, 21.

72. See, e.g., The Ohio State University Moritz College of Law, "Early Decision Option," accessed February 15, 2017, from http://moritzlaw.osu.edu/admissions/jd/applying/early-decision-option/. See also Shawn P. O'Connor, "Pros and Cons of Applying Early Decision to Law School," *U.S. News & World Report* (September 10, 2012), accessed August 9, 2016, from www.usnews.com/education/blogs/law-admissions-lowdown/2012/09/10/pros-and-cons-of-applying-early-decision-to-law-school.

73. In addition to admits, rejections, or wait list decisions, some schools use "administrative holds" (indicating a school could not make a decision within a certain time period in the admissions cycle, but signaling that an admission is a possibility later on). Montauk, *How to Get into the Top Law Schools*, 419–431. See also Shawn P. O'Connor, "5 Tips for Getting off the Law School Wait List," *U.S. News & World Report* (March 4, 2013), accessed August 10, 2016, from www.usnews.com/education/blogs/law-admissions-lowdown/2013/03/04/5-tips-for-getting-off-the-law-school-wait-list.

3 Law School

Students who have thoroughly prepared their law school applications are likely to discover that actually being in law school is not as shocking as it could be, at least at first. The old adage that "the first year of law school scares you to death, the second works you to death, and the third bores you to death" is certainly true for many students.[1] Still, beyond the rhetoric and what students see as the legal profession through popular fictional representations, few undergraduates will truly understand the nature of graduate law study until they are actually in law school.

Unlike undergraduate education, the assignments for the first day of class will be posted in advance, and professors will expect them to be read beforehand. Also, law schools typically test their students at the end of the semester through essay examinations that mimic the type of legal reasoning that is needed to pass the bar. That fact makes it extremely important to know how the tests are administered (i.e., when and in what format, such as essay, multiple choice, or both), especially in the crucial first year, since grades determine class ranking and, most likely, whether students are asked to join a school's law review (a highly prestigious student-run organization that publishes law review articles). In accordance with establishing a class ranking system, professors use an informal or mandatory grading curve, which will result in many scores going below expectations and, in the process, create significant barriers to make law review and, for some students, come as a real shock after an undergraduate experience filled with positive grading outcomes. There are no midterms and, for the most part, few writing assignments, except in legal writing and clinically based courses.[2] Also, students will discover that it is important to find a peer group early on, and to learn how to create (or buy commercial) outlines for final examination study, a process that can be not only intimidating for shy students but also devastating if the group study plan does not work out as expected.

Virtually all law schools have identical curricula and teaching methods, with plenty of opportunities to do extracurricular activities such as law review, mock trials, legal fraternities, and student organizations. As with any educational environment, it is essential to develop mentoring relationships with the faculty and key administrative staff, such as financial aid and career services personnel, and to discover if the law school has in place bar intervention courses or programs that help students prepare for the bar examination.[3] Even before going to law school, it is essential to know which courses are critical to bar study and to make careful selections about which electives to take in terms of knowing which ones are likely to appear on the bar examination. Similarly, it is wise early on to become familiar with the state's bar requirements, which differ state-by-state, and to work toward a mindset that it is absolutely necessary to pass the bar on the first sitting. While repeat bar examinations are a fact of life, another reality is that the job that was lined up after graduation might not be there in the event of an initial bar examination failure.[4]

Like any graduate education, law school will be a demanding and challenging test of individual fortitude, perseverance, and resilience. It will be a personal journey that is best accomplished by a complete dedication to the task at hand and a smart approach to handling the workload and new student or life responsibilities. In this light, it is important to get acclimated to the new study environment as quickly as possible. Accordingly, this chapter addresses what students can expect to discover while attending law school. The history of U.S. legal instruction is outlined first by describing past approaches and then by discussing the traditional method by which lawyers are trained today—the casebook method. Next, it details the type of curriculum that law schools typically offer to their students, using a three-year full time juris doctor degree program as a template for discussion. Thereafter, the chapter turns to explaining how lawyers become licensed to practice law in relation to bar admission trends.

THE CASEBOOK METHOD:
"LEARNING TO THINK LIKE A LAWYER"

Before the birth of modern law schools, lawyers were taught their craft through apprenticeships. Originating from the English legal system and transplanted to the American colonies, students learned how to practice law by studying it under the tutelage of an experienced lawyer in his law office after paying a fee. The practitioner's prestige usually determined how much the apprentice had to pay, which mostly permitted access to the law office's library but, oftentimes, little else, especially if the experienced attorney was too busy to supply actual legal training. Although some of the most important political statesmen in American history and law served as legal apprentices, including John Marshall, Thomas Jefferson, Joseph Story, and Daniel Webster, critics argued that it was a flawed method of legal training, in part because there was never a guarantee that the mentor was a competent instructor or that the pupil would gain much practical legal instruction. Thus, apprenticeships were not especially revered, simply because the legal tasks that were performed were nothing more than busywork provided by cheap labor. In addition, there were few incentives and little time to invest in learning legal theory or the broader principles of law that informed legal practice. As one legal historian put it, lawyers in the formative era of American legal practice "mastered the law not because of their legal apprenticeship, but in spite of it."[5]

Notably, while a few states still allow apprenticeships as part of their licensing requirements (discussed later in this chapter), for the most part they have been replaced by formal legal instruction in an academic university setting. With few exceptions, for full-time study all of the remaining states require a legal education by earning a juris doctor (JD) degree in a three-year period that is granted by an American Bar Association–accredited law school.[6] While many states do not permit the bar examination to be taken unless a JD is granted from an ABA-accredited school, a few states allow non-ABA law school graduates to sit for the bar. Yet, in 2015, of the 3,014 nationwide non-ABA-approved law school bar takers, only 19 percent passed, whereas 64 percent of the 66,763 bar takers from ABA-approved schools were successful. Even so, a non-ABA-approved law school may cost less than its ABA-approved counterpart, so it may be a good option for some students who know they are going to practice in a bar-eligible state if they are willing to assume the risks of trying to pass the bar.[7]

In the traditional ABA-approved law school setting, legal training involves a variety of pedagogical methods: lectures, legal clinics, moot courts, externships, and legal research and writing exercises, among others. Still, the prevalent instructional tool is learning legal doctrine from casebooks that enable students to read edited judicial opinions from appellate courts. The casebook method, developed under the deanship of Christopher Columbus Langdell and the presidency of Charles W. Eliot at Harvard Law School from the 1870s to the turn of the century, is a reasoning process that facilitates the discovery of general principles of law from specific cases decided by appeals courts. As law professor Robin L. West describes it, legal questions are ultimately resolved deductively by first inductively using specific past precedents to identify general principles of law and then applying them to the case and facts at hand.[8] The casebook's orthodoxy thus envisions law as a science since lawyer-scientists logically use it to "derive correct legal judgments from a few fundamental principles and concepts" that are found in the printed casebooks of common law (or judge-made) decisions. For Langdell, the casebook methodology is "the shortest and the best, if not the only way of mastering the doctrine effectually," since it empowers lawyers to apply neutral (value-free) doctrinal rules to every new case that arises in the legal system.[9]

By eliminating the past convention of teaching law in universities solely by lecture, Langdell's scientific approach to the law revolutionized modern legal instruction. Under the casebook method, students learn the law by studying appellate judicial opinions, reprinted in edited form in casebooks. Scientifically studying case law facilitated logical reasoning or, in popular terms, "thinking like a lawyer." Rather than simply give the black letter, or fixed rules, of law, professors point students toward the cases and allow the students to derive the law themselves. As explained next, a formal Socratic method is used in conjunction with the casebook analysis "to get to the foundations of students' . . . views by asking continual questions until a contradiction [is] exposed, thus proving the fallacy of the initial assumption."[10] By answering the professor's question, the student learns how to think like a lawyer.

In time, the reasoning process the casebook method embodies was transformed into a "case dialogue" instructional technique that is characterized by a Socratic style of questioning and answering by law professors and students in a classroom setting. Typically, the case dialogue helps indoctrinate first-year law students to the unique rigors and demanding challenges of law study, thereby socializing them into the legal profession by developing an analytical skill that is unique to licensed practitioners. Often in a large room with the seats arranged in a semi-circle, the law professor at the front of the class "asks questions of one student at a time, waiting for answers and then following up with the same student, asking more questions, one after another." Throughout the class session, the instructor systematically engages in a one-on-one questioning and answering dialogue with students who are constantly reminded to "read aloud the precise wording of a contract or a legal ruling given in the large book of legal cases that forms the text for the course." By definition, teaching in a doctrine-heavy format places the teacher in a dominant role and one that also limits full participation by the other members of the class who are not in the crosshairs of the law professor. In theory, the case dialogue method strengthens not only a student's substantive knowledge of doctrinal principles of law, but it also creates the type of analytical problem-solving skills that lawyers need to know in making judgments about what the law means or how to apply it in everyday practice. While critics observe that a growing number of law schools are tinkering with improving the utility of the Socratic method, the format is likely to persist for the foreseeable future without much change, especially since it is the way many law faculty were taught when they were students, and delivering it in large classes remains economically useful for law school administrations.[11]

For the lay public, the case method of instruction has become fictionalized in best-selling books and TV shows like John Jay Osborn Jr.'s *Paper Chase* and Scott Turow's *One L*. The concept of "cold calling," or when a law professor randomly picks on students to ask them questions about a reading or a short summary brief of the case that they may have prepared for class, reinforces the negative stereotyping that the case dialogue method generates in popular lore.[12] In the worst-case scenario, a student who is unprepared for class may be intimidated, and put to shame, by the relentless questioning of the law professor who treats the exercise like "a destructive tournament where gladiators of unequal power and experience vie to the death." While some law professors may adopt this style of pedagogical interrogation, many others do not; rather, they perceive using the Socratic and casebook methods as a positive learning experience to achieve the goal of learning how to problem-solve, reason by analogy, and critique or evaluate legal arguments or the law's impact.[13] As some educators suggest, learning how to "brief a case" properly in advance of class is an effective strategy for law students to adopt in overcoming any anxiety that might be generated by a law professor's use of the case dialogue instructional method of legal doctrine.[14]

In the end, students aiming to think like a lawyer must learn to master how to identify the appropriate rule of law in light of the relevant case facts, the first step in drawing analogies from precedents and reaching legal conclusions. The merit of an argument relies largely on the reliability of a lawyer's case analysis and a prediction as to which rule or interpretation applies in forming the conclusion. Often, however, the legal reasoning process will only reveal that there is not a clear-cut rule to be applied in every case since there might be multiple legal principles or interpretations that could apply in any given factual situation, thus forcing lawyers to make legal arguments that demonstrate to the court that a particular rule or analogy is the one that is best suited to resolve the legal problem at hand.[15] In this light, law students have used certain study techniques, such as IRAC (Issue, Rule, Application, and Conclusion) and CREAC (Conclusion, Rule, Explanation of Rule, Application, and Conclusion) methodologies, to help them deduce from general principles of law specific legal conclusions about how legal problems should be solved through case analysis. Still, for some educators, those learning strategies arguably have limited appeal or impact because they do not promote active learning, and they are applied to a law school curriculum that has largely remained unmodified from its original form in most law schools since the time Langdell and Eliot introduced the casebook method in the 1870s.[16]

THE LAW SCHOOL CURRICULUM

While some law schools are experimenting with their curricula and grading formats, in general there is little variation in what law schools offer in their course requirements to earn a law degree, in part due to the American Bar Association rules that establish certain threshold admission, curriculum, faculty, and educational resources criteria. Other factors, such as competitive pressures, the desire to replicate what top-tier law schools do, and the need to cover course material that is relevant to bar passage, also do not provide any incentives for law schools to go beyond well-established and traditional educational norms to remain the status quo. The lack of incentives to change what has worked in the past is especially true for the higher-ranked law schools, since the market for their wares usually remains constant. But, for many mid- to lower-ranked schools, economic realities increase the likelihood that it is necessary to adjust the curriculum to cater to market preferences in an effort to attract students and keep a constant revenue stream in place. Thus, on balance, law schools are reluctant to innovate or experiment with their basic course offerings. For these reasons and others, the core curriculum in law schools today closely resembles what has been taught in law schools across the nation for over 130 years, especially in the first year of study. As explained next, the key elements of a U.S. law curriculum feature lessons in legal doctrine, reading appellate court opinions through the case-book method, lecture and case dialogue instruction, and measurement of student performance by end-of-semester examinations that determine the bulk of student grades and class rankings.[17]

In accordance with the Langdellian casebook method, legal training is highly focused on teaching legal doctrine, as established by judges in the common law tradition. First-year students, or 1Ls, labor to learn the intricacies of certain subjects: contract, tort, property law, civil procedure, criminal law, legal research and writing, and, many times, constitutional law (see Table 3.1). Most first-year courses are based in the private law and common law, with little attention on how the bulk of law in the United States is made, which is through statutory and administrative law created by the political processes, namely legislatures, executives, and administrative agencies. Nor is the first year interdisciplinary in nature, which means that *how* certain social science and humanities subjects, such as political science, history, economics, psychology, or sociology, among others, impact the law is virtually ignored in the standard law school education. In addition, the first-year curriculum largely concentrates on teaching substantive legal doctrine and few practical or procedural skills. With the exception of civil procedure and the legal research and writing courses (and sometimes the insertion of a first-year "legal methods or practice" course that acquaints students with the legal system or judicial process), acquiring knowledge about legal procedure or learning "practice ready" legal skills is minimized because that subject matter is often taught through the lens of casebook study or judicial decision making.[18]

Intuitively, the first-year curriculum is structured to cover many of the core topics that are featured on the Multistate Bar Exam (discussed in this chapter's next section). While many scholars and legal professionals criticize the traditional law school curriculum for being guilty of "teaching to the test," some reformers argue that it might be advantageous for instructors to incorporate into the doctrinal

Table 3.1   Standard First-Year Curriculum in Law School

Course	Type of Law	Content
Contract law	Private law	Enforceability of private agreements
Tort law	Private law	Imposition of liability for unreasonable acts between private individuals that proximately cause harm
Property law	Private law	Facilitation of the various legal relationships affecting the possession and transfer of real (land) or personal (tangible items) property
Criminal law	Public law	Enforcement of public moral code through sanction
Constitutional law	Public law	Interpretation of constitutional documents
Civil procedure	Procedural law (mostly dealing in private law subject matter)	Rules of legal procedure developed by courts relative to federal civil cases and litigation
Legal research and writing	Practice-ready skills in public and private law contexts	Legal research and writing strategies and skills

Source: Derived from Christopher P. Banks and David M. O'Brien, *The Judicial Process: Law, Courts, and Judicial Politics* (Thousand Oaks, Calif.: Sage/CQ Press, 2015), 14 (Table 1.2); Sheldon Krantz, *The Legal Profession: What Is Wrong and How to Fix It* (New Providence, N.J.: LexisNexis, 2014), 20–21.

courses "bar exam skills" that build bar preparation while attending law school— these include encouraging active learning techniques that highlight regular writing, multiple-choice formats, and feedback opportunities.[19]

After the first year, students have a wider variety of elective choices in course offerings, which may not necessarily be on the bar exam but afford the opportunity to learn specific areas in the legal field. Becoming acquainted with discrete areas of the law is a first step in contemplating what type of expertise students want to develop in a specialized field, an occupational decision that most lawyers will make in creating a professional niche after passing the bar if they go into legal practice. While there are some exceptions, many law schools favor an unstructured elective system that gives students free rein to choose the courses that interest them the most in accordance with their anticipated career path and professional objectives. Still, some schools try to influence the students' decision making by recommending what courses they should take, including the necessity to fulfill the ABA requirement of taking an upper-level writing and professional responsibility class (the latter of which is geared toward passing the Multistate Professional Responsibility Exam, a precondition for taking most state bar examinations, discussed in the next section). The recommended doctrinal courses typically focus on business regulation and trial advocacy topics. Thus, for the second year, many law schools advise their students to take Administrative Law, Corporations (or Business Organizations), Federal Taxation, and Evidence (which is covered on the Multistate Bar Exam), though students also have the chance to fill their schedules with other popular courses, such as Criminal Procedure, Wills and Estates, Family Law (or Domestic Relations), and Employment (or Labor) Law. While some schools offer practice-ready courses or opportunities such as clinical programs, externships, or extracurricular activities (joining legal fraternities and organizations, working as an unpaid intern in a local law firm or clerking for a judge, or participating in mock trial, moot court, and trial advocacy programs), typically students elect to reserve them for the third and final year in law school.[20]

The institutional structure and delivery of legal education has been subject to long-standing criticisms about its pedagogical justification and its practical utility. While Chapter 5 explores these criticisms and reform proposals in depth, at present it is worth noting that in many respects the U.S. system of legal instruction stands apart from the rest of world in educating lawyers. Unlike many other global jurisdictions, most aspiring lawyers in the United States must successfully complete seven years of academic study before becoming eligible to practice law.[21] Once they finish a four-year undergraduate degree (which, notably, does not require any prelaw instruction), students then earn a three-year graduate degree in law as a condition to sitting for the bar examination.

Although some countries, such as Australia, Japan, and South Korea, are receptive to modeling legal instruction in the mold of a graduate degree, in Europe and elsewhere the general secondary training of students at the high school level qualifies them to enroll directly in a university program in a specific academic discipline, including law or medicine, without having to complete an additional graduate degree as a precondition to entering the legal profession or professoriate. In such places, an undergraduate degree functions as a law degree. Moreover, the United States is differentiated from other countries by (1) requiring a bar examination after law school graduation; (2) teaching law as an academic discipline with tenure-track faculty who often have not earned an advanced PhD, but only a three-year JD (law) degree; (3) providing legal training to students with faculty who have no, or scant, experience in practicing law even though the bulk of law school graduates enter into legal practice, especially in top-rated law schools; and (4) allowing academic legal scholarship, which is grounded in publishing in student-led law review journals that have considerable discretion to accept and publish journal articles, to use a non-peer-review process that heavily determines elite job placement opportunities for students and also goes a long way in influencing whether law professors receive tenure or build a reputable academic career in the legal profession.[22]

LICENSING REQUIREMENTS AND BAR ADMISSIONS

Despite institutional and financial constraints, thousands of law graduates are admitted into legal practice each year. In 2015, nearly 80,000 people took the bar exam, and a little less than 60 percent, 45,993, successfully entered the legal marketplace.[23] Over 1.3 million attorneys were licensed in the United States in 2016, a demographic that was bolstered by a steady increase in new law schools (from 135 to 201) and enrollments (from 49,552 to 150,113) between the 1960s and 2013. Although law school applications and bar passage rates have declined in recent years, in 2015 nearly 350,000 people across the United States applied to law school, and almost 40,000 matriculated in the fall semester as 1Ls. In line with past trends, it is still reasonable to expect that the demand for legal education will remain constant and that roughly 40,000 to 50,000 law graduates will be admitted into legal practice each year in the foreseeable future.[24]

Shaping the content of and administering bar examinations is the responsibility of state bar admitting authorities that remain under the general supervision of the court of last resort in the relevant jurisdiction. While law schools are cognizant of bar requirements, there is little evidence that they structure their curriculum around the law subjects that are tested on bar examinations, at least in regard to second- and third-year course offerings.[25] In this respect, the disjunction between law school curricula and bar examination criteria, along with differences in state law and the diversity of state judiciaries, creates a system of bar eligibility that varies widely. Still, the most conventional way to gain bar eligibility and admission is by graduating from an ABA-accredited law school. While eligibility and admission are possible through other means, such as apprenticeship or engaging in study at a non-ABA-accredited law school, the low bar passage rates that are linked to those methods suggest that attending an ABA-accredited institution is more likely to produce a better bar examination outcome for most students.[26]

As an alternative to going to law school, a few jurisdictions—namely California, Vermont, Virginia, and Washington—license lawyers after completing only an apprenticeship (through law office study). The conditions for bar eligibility, though, differ considerably in apprenticeship-licensing states. In Virginia, applicants must enroll in Law Reader, a program that requires three years of law office study with a supervising attorney who has ten years of legal practice experience and can mentor for at least twenty-five hours per week over forty weeks of the year. Similarly, with the payment of a $1,500 annual fee, Washington's Law Clerk Program requires apprentice law clerks to be employed, and study, in a law office for thirty-two hours per week over a four-year period under the supervision of an attorney with ten years of experience. California and Vermont's apprenticeship programs, on the other hand, stipulate four years of law office study, but with attorneys who have five and three years of experience, respectively. Other states, such as Maine, New York, and Wyoming, permit applicants to sit for the bar if they complete a combination of law office and ABA-accredited law school study; and, in West Virginia, it is possible for applicants who attend a non-ABA-accredited law school for three years to take the bar examination if they complete an additional three years of law office training.[27]

Apart from apprenticeships, Wisconsin is the only state that grants bar admission by diploma privilege (after graduating from one of the two state law schools), although New Hampshire has an analogous alternative licensing program that permits its students to go directly into practice through its Daniel Webster Scholar Honors Program.[28] While several states offer bar eligibility to applicants graduating from foreign law schools or non-ABA-accredited law schools, the bar passage rates relative to those admission criteria remain low in comparison to the rates from ABA-accredited law schools.[29]

Accordingly, with few exceptions, aspiring lawyers typically prepare and sit for a state-specific bar examination in most law-licensing jurisdictions once they graduate from an ABA-accredited law school. Even so, the fact that a majority of law graduates in the United States have to take the additional step of passing a bar examination is an anomaly in relation to global legal education systems because many countries authorize entry into the legal profession by simply completing a law degree (although sometimes in combination with fulfilling practice-based apprenticeships and mentoring requirements, or other criteria). In this light, critics and reformers argue that licensing lawyers through a bar examination is superfluous and even damaging to students because (1) bar exams do not test the skills that are required for law practice, (2) they test a wide assortment of subject matter that is not always taught as required courses in law schools, and (3) studying for them often requires taking commercial bar preparation courses that are cost prohibitive, especially when some students have already expended several hundred thousand dollars to attend law school, often through onerous student loan debt.[30]

Furthermore, critics point to declining bar passage rates in recent years as another sign that law schools are increasingly forced due to economic pressures to enroll students who are unqualified to pass the bar if they manage to graduate (see Figure 3.1). Even the president of the National Conference of Bar Examiners (NCBE), the organization that constructs and tallies the scores of bar examinations that are used across the nation, lamented that "all [indicators] point to the fact that the group that sat in July 2014 was less able than the group that sat in July 2013."

Figure 3.1   Ten-Year Bar Passage Rates, 2006–2015

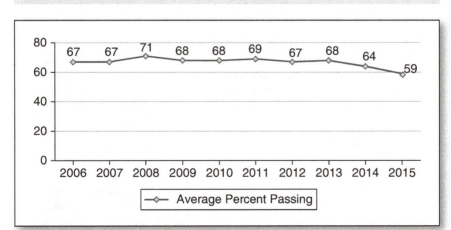

Source: National Conference of Bar Examiners, "2015 Statistics," *The Bar Examiner* 85 (March 2016).

Still, some law deans, such as Stephen C. Ferruolo of the University of San Diego School of Law, counter that the NCBE is at fault, contending that the exam, as constructed, "is an unpredictable and unacceptable impediment for accessibility to the legal profession." In theory, the test is designed to protect the public against admitting unqualified lawyers; yet, in practice, the bar examination cannot escape the long-standing criticism that it is expensive and time-consuming and, since it only tests recalling legal doctrine, does "nothing to measure lawyering skills."[31]

Notwithstanding the vitriol, most law graduates go through the traditional ritual of preparing for, and successfully completing, state-specific bar examinations that are constructed in different formats and administered by the NCBE and the relevant jurisdiction (see Table 3.2). In virtually all locales, applicants must pass a national ethics test, the Multistate Professional Responsibility Examination (MPRE), in addition to passing the bar examination. Administered three times a year, the MPRE is significant because it evaluates whether lawyers understand the Model Rules of Professional Conduct, the professional ethical rules that are promulgated by the American Bar Association and implemented in some form in every state.[32] For bar examinations, which are offered in February and July, most jurisdictions use a two-day testing period that, on the first day, administers a national standardized multiple-choice test, the Multistate Bar Examination (MBE). The MBE evaluates competencies that are addressed in many first-year law courses. On the second day, jurisdictions test a wide range of legal substantive and procedural subject matter either through written essays that are created by the state bar licensing authority or, increasingly, with the NCBE-based Multistate Essay Examination (MEE) and the Multistate Performance Test (MPT).[33]

In response to the denunciation that bar licensing is too parochial and impedes cross-jurisdictional practice across state lines, a growing number of states are adopting the Uniform Bar Examination (UBE) as the bar examination of choice. With the UBE, the score that is established after taking the MEE, two MPT tasks,

Table 3.2   Bar Examination Testing Purposes and Formats

Test/Jurisdictions	Purpose	Format
Multistate Professional Responsibility Examination (MPRE) • Used since 1980 • All jurisdictions except Wisconsin and Puerto Rico	Evaluate knowledge and understanding of ethical codes of conduct	60 multiple-choice questions testing client–lawyer relationship, client confidentiality, conflicts of interest, competence, legal malpractice/civil liability, litigation/advocacy, transactions/communications about legal services, lawyers' public duties, and judicial conduct

Test/Jurisdictions	Purpose	Format
Multistate Bar Examination (MBE) • Used since 1972 • All jurisdictions except Louisiana • Each jurisdiction determines its own policy relative to weight given to MBE and other scores; but Uniform Bar Examination jurisdictions weigh MBE 50%	Evaluate application of basic legal principles and legal reasoning to analyze fact patterns in different situations	200 multiple-choice questions testing civil procedure, constitutional law, contracts, criminal law and procedure, evidence, real property, and torts (most first-year law school subjects)
Multistate Essay Examination (MEE) • Used since 1988 • 35 jurisdictions • Each jurisdiction determines its own policy relative to weight given to MEE and other scores; but Uniform Bar Examination jurisdictions weigh MEE 30%	Evaluate ability to spot legal issues and analyze them by using legal reasoning and legal principles in hypothetical factual situations	Six 30-minute written essays testing subjects as determined by relevant jurisdiction, including business associations, civil procedure, conflict of laws, constitutional law, contracts, criminal law and procedure, evidence, family law, real property, secured transactions (UCC Article 9), torts, and trusts and estates
Multistate Performance Test (MPT) • Used since 1997 • 41 jurisdictions • Each jurisdiction determines its own policy relative to weight given to MPT and other scores; but Uniform Bar Examination jurisdictions weigh MPT 20%	Evaluate use of basic lawyering skills in realistic situations by determining if applicant can complete a task a beginning lawyer should be able to finish	Two written 90-minute items • A jurisdiction may select one or both items as part of its bar examination • Jurisdictions using Uniform Bar Examination use two MPTs as part of their bar examinations

Source: National Conference of Bar Examiners, "2015 Statistics," *The Bar Examiner* 85 (March 2016).

and the MBE is generated by the adopting jurisdiction; but it is portable, or transferrable, to other UBE jurisdictions. In line with the heightened concern that law school graduates are not practice ready, the UBE incorporates the MEE and MPT components into the bar examination in an effort to evaluate more accurately if applicants are entering into the legal profession with sufficient practice skills and competencies. To illustrate, the MPT requires applicants to answer a question posed by a hypothetical case file that a lawyer might encounter in legal practice. Beyond its pedagogical purpose, the UBE is a practical and attractive option for law graduates who have not been able to find employment in a particular state or U.S. territory due to the economic downturn in the legal marketplace; and, the UBE creates more flexibility for lawyers who need to relocate or manage cases involving multiple jurisdictions or foreign countries. As then New York chief judge Jonathan Lippman explained in 2015, the legal profession is "sticking our heads in the sand if we don't realize the practice of law doesn't stop at state lines," so "there has to be portability with the law license around the country."[34]

A final hurdle that bar applicants must satisfy to become professionally licensed is completing the character and fitness requirements of the relevant jurisdiction. Under this criteria, bar applicants must submit to a thorough investigation of their personal background in order to determine if they are qualified to receive a professional credential and the public's trust. In the past, the American Bar Association used this morality requirement as the means to discriminate and exclude disfavored would-be practitioners (immigrants, social outcasts, and the impoverished) from entering the legal profession. Doing so served the ABA's interest of solidifying the social status, elitism, and independence of licensed lawyers. The modern justification is that it protects the public and the legal profession from the harm created by admitting persons who are unfit or unqualified to practice law.[35]

In accordance with prevailing norms, bar applicants prepare and complete the character and fitness requirement near the end of law school. Bar examiners begin their investigation by asking bar applicants to complete a lengthy questionnaire that details a wide range of personal information, including employment and educational histories, military service, civil litigation actions, prior illegal conduct, substance abuse problems, academic misfeasance, financial neglect, and psychological difficulties. Full disclosure is expected, and the questionnaires require applicants to provide documentation to support their written statements. Such documentation may include driving records, credit histories, and character references. If there are issues, bar examination committees will follow up by conducting a hearing in which applicants will have the opportunity to rebut the presumption that they are unfit to practice law. Applicants can do that by showing the committee that there are a variety of factors that establish, on the whole, good moral character and fitness, including facts addressing evidence of rehabilitation and whether the conduct at issue was an aberration in the past or not very serious. While many jurisdictions use their own forms and processes, many others delegate the inquiry to the National Conference of Bar Examiners, which compiles the relevant information and forwards it to the bar examination committee for review and decision.[36]

Regardless of the mechanism used, character and fitness investigations are controversial because they are highly invasive, discriminatory, time consuming, labor intensive, disruptive, and expensive for both the applicants and bar examination officials. At least some of these criticisms have prompted reform and revision. In 2014, some state bars adjusted the wording of their questionnaires after the Department of Justice alerted them that making inquiries about mental health status may discriminate against persons with disabilities on a variety of grounds and therefore violate federal law. For its part, the NCBE retired a question asking if applicants have been diagnosed or treated for "bipolar disorder, schizophrenia, paranoia or any other psychotic disorder" within the past five years and replaced it with one asking if applicants have "exhibited any conduct or behavior that could call into question your ability to practice law in a competent, ethical, and professional manner." In addition, academic studies have found that character and fitness tests have little predictive value in establishing the likelihood that bar applicants will actually engage in improper behavior as licensed professionals; and, on balance, very few applicants are denied bar admission on the grounds of character and fitness.[37]

CONCLUSION

A critic of the American legal profession characterizes it as "ponderous, backward-looking, and self-preservationist," with more than a little justification. Beset with problems of a depressed legal marketplace, the oversupply and underemployment of lawyers, inflated tuition rates, dubious recruitment practices, obstinate administration and law faculties, student loan abuses, and suspect pedagogical methods, legal education "is in the cross-hairs of multiple shooters: law firms and other legal employers; law clients (General Counsels and business people alike); prospective students; the *New York Times*; and so on."[38] Even President Barack Obama waded into the controversies by declaring in 2013 that "law schools would probably be wise to think about being two years instead of three years," since the law student's time is better spent acquiring legal practice experience by clerking or taking unpaid internships at law firms.[39] In response, law schools are being stressed not only by these forces but also by the organized bar and its accreditation and state bar licensing authorities to revisit long-standing educational norms by adjusting their cultures and making revisions to the structure or delivery of legal training with modifications to grading systems, curricula, and degree programs.

Although the process of effectuating any needed reforms is likely to take place slowly and on an incremental, piecemeal basis, if at all, law schools increasingly seem to be getting the message. Many law schools, including those that are top rated, have moved away from grading solely on the curve, and they are rethinking or revising their curricula by incorporating more practice-ready experiential and interdisciplinary courses, or adopting pedagogical learning techniques that are not solely based on the case dialogue method. Bar intervention courses have grown in popularity as well since they tend to help at-risk students to perform better on the bar examination. To illustrate, after an extensive review of its program, Harvard Law School announced that it no longer grades on the curve or has a class ranking system. In addition, it "recently undertook a sweeping overhaul of its first-year curriculum" by adding courses in legislation and regulation, as well as in international and comparative law. In its estimation, the new requirement, as well other innovations that offer students additional experiential courses that center on problem solving and dispute resolution, necessarily "reflects legal practice in the 21st century."[40]

Indisputably, the changes instituted at Harvard and elsewhere have the potential to set an example for other schools to follow in effectuating reform. Still, they underscore the challenges that some reformers claim law schools face in the future since they manifest the reality that law schools will only remain viable if they undertake other reforms that (1) reduce enrollments, tuition rates, and operating costs (by cutting back on their library resources, using fewer tenure-track faculty and more adjuncts with practice experience, for example); (2) give teaching a greater priority over research; and (3) increase diversity and innovation by adopting programs that will target nontraditional uses of legal education in the marketplace.[41] Some of the major reform issues and challenges that confront law schools and the legal profession as a whole are addressed more completely in the last chapter. Before then, the next chapter gives a synopsis of what law students might do once they graduate and enter into legal practice or other related fields of employment.

SELECTED READINGS

American Bar Association Task Force on the Future of Legal Education. *Report and Recommendations*. Chicago, Ill.: American Bar Association, January 2014.

Moliterno, James E. *The American Legal Profession in Crisis: Resistance and Responses to Change*. New York, N.Y.: Oxford University Press, 2013.

Stolker, Carel. *Rethinking the Law School: Education, Research, Outreach and Governance*. Cambridge, U.K.: Cambridge University Press, 2014.

West, Robin L. *Teaching Law: Justice, Politics, and the Demands of Professionalism*. New York, N.Y.: Cambridge University Press, 2015.

WEB LINKS

American Bar Association, "Bar Admissions" (www.americanbar.org/groups/legal_education/resources/bar_admissions.html)

National Conference of Bar Examiners and American Bar Association Section of Legal Education and Admissions to the Bar, *Comprehensive Guide to Bar Admission Requirements 2016* (www.ncbex.org/pubs/bar-admissions-guide/2016/index.html#p=1)

ENDNOTES

1. R. Michael Cassidy, "Reforming the Law School Curriculum from the Top Down," *Journal of Legal Education* 64 (2015): 428, 437.

2. Philip C. Kissam, "The Ideology of the Case Method/Final Examination Law School," *University of Cincinnati Law Review* 70 (2001): 137, 151–153. An analysis of the strengths and weaknesses of testing students by way of a three-hour final examination that is graded on a bell curve at the end of the semester is found in Philip C. Kissam, "Law School Examinations," *Vanderbilt Law Review* 42 (1989): 433–504. See also William M. Sullivan et al., *Educating Lawyers: Preparation for the Profession of Law (A Publication of the Carnegie Foundation for the Advancement of Teaching)* (San Francisco, Calif.: Jossey-Bass, 2007), 162–171. Data from a national study of law school performance show that first-year students are overly optimistic about the grades they will receive, before their

first set of exams. See Richard Sander and Jane Bambauer, "The Secret of My Success: How Status, Eliteness, and School Performance Shape Legal Careers," *Journal of Empirical Legal Studies* 9 (2012): 893, 901.

3. Especially in recent years, law schools have responded to increased pressure to generate enrollments by admitting students who are ill equipped to undertake law study, which, in turn, has led to the creation of academic programs that aid at-risk students to not only remain in law school, but also pass the bar examination. Aleatra P. Williams, "The Role of Bar Preparation Programs in the Current Legal Education Crisis," *Wayne Law Review* 59 (2013): 383, 395–396. While some schools offer bar preparation programs, others do not, so students often rely on expensive commercial bar review courses after law school to achieve bar success. See Mario W. Mainero, "We Should Not Rely on Commercial Bar Reviews to Do Our Job: Why Labor-Intensive Comprehensive Bar Examination Preparation Can and Should Be a Part of the Law School Mission," *Chapman Law Review* 19 (2016): 545–555, 573–581 (discussing Fowler School of Law's bar preparation program, and reporting that the cost among sixteen different commercial programs varies from $500 to $7,500); and Scott Johns, "Empirical Reflections: A Statistical Evaluation of Bar Exam Program Interventions," *University of Louisville Law Review* 54 (2016): 35–72 (describing the success of University of Denver Sturm College of Law bar passage program).

4. See Commission on Bar Admissions and Lawyer Performance and Richard A. White, "AALS Survey of Law Schools on Programs and Courses Designed to Enhance Bar Examination Performance," *Journal of Legal Education* 52 (2002): 453, 455 (observing that students failing the bar will not easily find employment).

5. Charles R. McKirdy, "The Lawyer as Apprentice: Legal Education in Eighteenth Century Massachusetts," *Journal of Legal Education* 28 (1976): 134–135; American Bar Association Section of Legal Education and Admissions to the Bar, *Legal Education and Professional Development—An Educational Continuum (Report of the Task Force on Law Schools and the Profession: Narrowing the Gap)* (Chicago, Ill.: American Bar Association, 1992), 103–104.

6. Accreditation standards evolved from the efforts of the American Bar Association, the Association of American Law Schools, and local bar associations. The accreditation standards, as well as other requirements—such as making college study a prerequisite for law school admission, requiring attendance in law schools for three years, and making graduation a precondition for taking bar examinations—allowed the legal profession to become highly autonomous and self-regulating (discussed in Chapter 5). Robert Stevens, *Law School: Legal Education in America from the 1850s to the 1980s* (Chapel Hill: University of North Carolina Press, 1983), 94–95, 105 (n. 23).

7. Menachem Wecker, "Weigh the Benefits, Disadvantages of Attending a Non-ABA Law School," *U.S. News & World Report* (December 17, 2012), accessed July 18, 2016, from www .usnews.com/education/best-graduate-schools/top-law-schools/articles/2012/12/17/ weigh-the-benefits-disadvantages-of-attending-a-non-aba-law-school. See also National Conference of Bar Examiners, "2015 Statistics," accessed July 18, 2016, from www.ncbex .org/pdfviewer/?file=%2Fdmsdocument%2F195, 19.

8. Robin L. West, *Teaching Law: Justice, Politics, and the Demands of Professionalism* (New York, N.Y.: Cambridge University Press, 2015), 30.

9. As quoted from Landgell's *Contracts* casebook in Stevens, *Law School*, 52. See also Thomas C. Grey, "Langdell's Orthodoxy," *University of Pittsburgh Law Review* 45 (1983): 1, 5; and Anthony Chase, "The Birth of the Modern Law School," *The American Journal of Legal History* 23 (1979): 329–348.

10. Elizabeth Garrett, "The Role of the Socratic Method in Modern Law Schools," *Green Bag* (Winter 1998): 199–208.

11. Jamie R. Abrams, "Reframing the Socratic Method," *Journal of Legal Education* 64 (2015): 562, 564. American Bar Association Section of Legal Education and Admissions to the

Bar, *Legal Education and Professional Development*, 236–237. The quoted material is from a report issued by researchers who observed first-year classes in a study that critiqued law instruction: Sullivan et al., *Educating Lawyers*, 49–50. See also Melissa J. Marlow, "Does Kingsfield Live? Teaching with Authenticity in Today's Law Schools," *Journal of Legal Education* 65 (2015): 229, 233.

12. Tori Slatton, "The Law School Survival Guide: Cold Calling," *Thought Catalog* (April 8, 2014), accessed October 24, 2015, from http://thoughtcatalog.com/victoria-slatton/2014/04/law-school-survival-guide-cold-calling/.

13. The quoted portion is from law professor Elizabeth Garrett's defense of the Socratic method in "Role of the Socratic Method in Modern Law Schools," 201. In addition to a lecture style of instruction, other professors adopt an active learning strategy that involves more class participation and attentive feedback mechanisms. Michael Hunter Schwartz, Gerald F. Hess, and Sophie M. Sparrow, *What the Best Law Teachers Do* (Cambridge, Mass.: Harvard University Press, 2013), 205–207, 214–215.

14. A case brief is a short summary (a page or less) of each case that lists the most crucial information by headings: (1) case name and citation, (2) case facts (what happened in the case and how lower courts ruled on the case before it reached the appellate court), (3) the legal issue (what is in dispute), (4) the holding (what the appellate court decided and how it applied rule of law), and (5) the case rationale (the appellate court's reasoning behind its holding). See David M. O'Brien, *Constitutional Law and Politics: Struggles of Power and Government Accountability*, vol. 1 (New York, N.Y.: Norton, 2014), 1109. The concept of cold calling is discussed in Slatton, "Law School Survival Guide."

15. Kurt M. Saunders and Linda Levine, "Learning to Think like a Lawyer," *University of San Francisco Law Review* 29 (1994): 125–126.

16. Andrea J. Boyack, "More Talking, More Writing," *The Law Teacher* 22 (2016): 2–4, accessed February 16, 2017, from http://lawteaching.org/wp-content/uploads/2016/06/lawteacher2016spring.pdf. See also Diane B. Kraft, "CREAC in the Real World," *Cleveland State Law Review* 63 (2015): 567–597; and Gerald Lebovits, "Cracking the Code to Legal Arguments: From IRAC to CRARC to Combinations in Between," *New York State Bar Association Journal* 82 (2010): 64–68.

17. Sheldon Krantz, *The Legal Profession: What Is Wrong and How to Fix It* (New Providence, N.J.: LexisNexis, 2014), 20–21. See also Rick Glofcheski, "Rethinking Teaching, Learning and Assessment in the Twenty-First Century Law Curriculum," in *Legal Education in the Global Context: Opportunities and Challenges*, ed. Christopher Gane and Robin Hui Huang (Farnham, U.K.: Ashgate, 2015), 131–146; Cassidy, "Reforming the Law School Curriculum from the Top Down," 429–430.

18. West, *Teaching Law*, 96–98.

19. See Emmeline Paulette Reeves, "Teaching to the Test: The Incorporation of Elements of Bar Exam Preparation in Legal Education," *Journal of Legal Education* 64, no. 4 (May 2015): 645–655. All courses listed in Table 3.1 are tested on the Multistate Bar Exam and state bar examinations. National Conference of Bar Examiners, "Preparing for the MBE," accessed July 21, 2016, from www.ncbex.org/exams/mbe/preparing/.

20. While there is variation among law schools, the second and third years are more flexible and less doctrinal. Law School Admission Council, "Thinking about Law School: Is There a Standard Law School Curriculum?," accessed July 23, 2016, from http://lsac.org/jd/thinking-about-law-school/standard-curriculum. See, e.g., New York Law School, "Required Courses," accessed July 23, 2016, from www.nyls.edu/academics/j_d-course_of_study/sequence_of_courses/; and Cornell Law School, "2L and 3L," accessed July 23, 2016, from www.lawschool.cornell.edu/admissions/degrees/jd/2l_3l.cfm.

21. Carel Stolker, *Rethinking the Law School: Education, Research, Outreach and Governance* (Cambridge, U.K.: Cambridge University Press, 2014), 1–2.

22. Ibid., 1–2, 16–19.

23. National Conference of Bar Examiners, "2015 Statistics," 16.

24. Graduating class sizes have declined since 2013, but nationally the average yearly class size between 2006 and 2015 was 44,074. National Association of Law Placement, "Salaries for New Graduates Rise While Employment Rate Remains Unchanged, Number of Private Practice Jobs Tumbles," accessed September 14, 2016, from www.nalp.org/2015_select edfindings_pr. From 2011 to 2015, an average of 53,093 persons passed the bar exam in the United States. See the statistical summaries of bar applicant passage rates in the March issues between 2011 and 2016, in National Conference of Bar Examiners, *The Bar Examiner*, accessed July 26, 2016, from www.ncbex.org/publications/the-bar-examiner/. See also American Bar Association Section of Legal Education and Admissions to the Bar, "Enrollment and Degrees Awarded, 1963–2012 Academic Years," accessed July 26, 2016, from www.americanbar.org/content/dam/aba/administrative/legal_education_ and_admissions_to_the_bar/statistics/enrollment_degrees_awarded.authcheckdam.pdf; and American Bar Association, "ABA National Lawyer Population Survey: Historical Trend in Total National Lawyer Population, 1878–2016," accessed July 26, 2016, from www.americanbar.org/content/dam/aba/administrative/market_research/total-national-lawyer-population-1878-2016.authcheckdam.pdf.

25. To illustrate, one study found that less than half of law schools required Business Associations and Trusts and Estates as courses in their curriculum even though a large majority of state bar examinations tested those subjects. However, newly accredited schools (after 2002) tended to structure their programs around bar passage. Catherine L. Carpenter, "Recent Trends in Law School Curricula: Findings from the 2010 ABA Curriculum Study," *The Bar Examiner* 85 (2012): 6, 11. See also Brent Newton, "The Ninety-Five Theses: Systemic Reforms of American Legal Education and Licensure," *South Carolina Law Review* 64 (2012): 55, 133.

26. On average, in 2015, 64 percent of applicants passed the bar when graduating from an ABA-accredited law school. See note 24 for the bar passage rates in respect to other methods of bar eligibility.

27. Sean Patrick Farrell, "The Lawyer's Apprentice: How to Learn the Law without Law School," *New York Times* (July 30, 2014), accessed July 25, 2016, from www.nytimes .com/2014/08/03/education/edlife/how-to-learn-the-law-without-law-school.html?_r=0. See also Sustainable Economies Law Center, "A State-by-State Guide to Apprenticeships," *Like Lincoln: Becoming a Lawyer without Going to Law School* (2013), accessed July 25, 2016, from http://likelincoln.org/state-by-state-guide-to-apprenticeships/.

28. Sarah Valentine, "Flourish or Founder: The New Regulatory Regime in Legal Education," *Journal of Law and Education* 44 (2015): 473, 480–481, 515–524. In Wisconsin, a diploma privilege is afforded to graduates of the University of Wisconsin Law School and Marquette University Law School. Board of Bar Examiners, "Admission to the Practice of Law in Wisconsin: Diploma Privilege 2017," accessed February 16, 2017, from www .wicourts.gov/services/attorney/bardiploma.htm. Each jurisdiction's bar requirements are found in National Conference of Bar Examiners and American Bar Association Section of Legal Education and Admissions to the Bar, *Comprehensive Guide to Bar Admission Requirements 2016*, accessed July 25, 2016, from www.ncbex.org/pubs/bar-admissions-guide/2016/index.html#p=1.

29. In 2015, for applicants graduating from a foreign law school, only 28 percent passed the bar. For non-ABA-accredited schools, the bar passage rate was 20 percent for conventional, or fixed-facility, schools that instruct mostly in physical classroom facilities; 20 percent for correspondence schools that instruct students by correspondence; and 17 percent for online institutions that provide interactive classes and instruction over the Internet. National Conference of Bar Examiners, "2015 Statistics," 19, 28; Board of Bar Examiners, "Admission to the Practice of Law in Wisconsin."

30. James E. Moliterno, *The American Legal Profession in Crisis: Resistance and Responses to Change* (New York, N.Y.: Oxford University Press, 2013), 229–223. See also Stolker, *Rethinking the Law School*, 18.

31. All quotes in this paragraph are from Elizabeth Olson, "Bar Exam, the Standard to Become a Lawyer, Comes under Fire," *New York Times* (March 19, 2015), accessed July 26, 2016, from www.nytimes.com/2015/03/20/business/dealbook/bar-exam-the-standard-to-become-a-lawyer-comes-under-fire.html.

32. American Bar Association, "Model Rules of Professional Conduct: Table of Contents," accessed July 26, 2016, from www.americanbar.org/groups/professional_responsibility/publications/model_rules_of_professional_conduct/model_rules_of_professional_conduct_table_of_contents.html. A listing of states and the date of adoption of the model rules are found in American Bar Association, "State Adoption of the ABA Model Rules of Professional Conduct," accessed July 26, 2016, from www.americanbar.org/groups/professional_responsibility/publications/model_rules_of_professional_conduct/alpha_list_state_adopting_model_rules.html. For a description of Watergate's legacy in affecting professional ethics, see Deborah L. Rhode, *Lawyers as Leaders* (New York, N.Y.: Oxford University Press, 2013), 96–98; see also National Conference of Bar Examiners, "Jurisdictions Requiring the MPRE," accessed July 26, 2016, from www.ncbex.org/exams/mpre/.

33. American Bar Association, "Bar Admissions," accessed July 26, 2016, from www.americanbar.org/groups/legal_education/resources/bar_admissions.html.

34. Stephanie Clifford and James C. McKinley Jr., "New York to Adopt a Uniform Bar Exam Used in 15 Other States," *New York Times* (May 5, 2015), accessed July 26, 2016, from www.nytimes.com/2015/05/06/nyregion/new-york-state-to-adopt-uniform-bar-exam.html?_r=0. For a listing of UBE jurisdictions, see National Conference of Bar Examiners, "Jurisdictions That Have Adopted the UBE," accessed July 26, 2016, from www.ncbex.org/exams/ube/.

35. Leslie C. Levin, Christine Zozula, and Peter Siegelman, "The Questionable Character of the Bar's Character and Fitness Inquiry," *Law & Social Inquiry* 40 (2015): 51–52. See also Moliterno, *American Legal Profession in Crisis*, 25–27.

36. Levin et al., "Questionable Character of the Bar's Character and Fitness Inquiry," 51–55. The NCBE's character and fitness service, and a sample questionnaire, is detailed in National Conference of Bar Examiners, "Character and Fitness Investigations," accessed July 27, 2016, from http://ncbex.org/character-and-fitness/.

37. Levin et al., "Questionable Character of the Bar's Character and Fitness Inquiry," 51–55. See also Anna Stolley Persky, "State Bars May Probe Applicants' Behavior, but Not Mental Health Status, Says DOJ," *ABA Journal* (June 1, 2014): 1.

38. James E. Moliterno, "The Future of Legal Education Reform," *Pepperdine Law Review* 40 (2013): 423, 427.

39. Peter Lattman, "Obama Says Law School Should Be Two, Not Three, Years," *New York Times* (August 23, 2013), accessed July 27, 2016, from http://dealbook.nytimes.com/2013/08/23/obama-says-law-school-should-be-two-years-not-three/.

40. Harvard Law School, "J.D. Program," accessed July 27, 2016, from http://hls.harvard.edu/dept/academics/degree-programs/j-d-program/; Harvard Law School, "HLS Grading Policy," accessed July 27, 2016, from http://hls.harvard.edu/dept/ocs/employers/hls-grading-policy/. See also Karen Tokarz et al., "Legal Education at a Crossroads: Innovation, Integration, and Pluralism Required!," *Washington University Journal of Law & Policy* 43 (2013): 11, 32 (n. 95).

41. Thomas W. Lyons, "Legal Education: Learning What Lawyers Need," in *The Relevant Lawyer: Reimagining the Future of the Legal Profession*, ed. Paul A. Haskins (Chicago, Ill.: ABA Standing Committee on Professionalism, Center for Professional Responsibility, 2015), 221, 225. See, generally, West, *Teaching Law*, 208–215.

4 The Practice of Law

Tens of thousands of law graduates are admitted into legal practice each year. Although bar admission rates have declined in recent years, they do not show any meaningful sign of diminishing significantly over the long term. In the short term, changes in the legal marketplace have slowed the pace of juris doctor (JD) enrollments and Law School Admission Test (LSAT) administrations, due in large part to the negative effects of the 2008 recession (see Figure 4.1). But, given the steady rate

Figure 4.1   Bar Admission, JD Enrollment, and LSAT Administration Trends

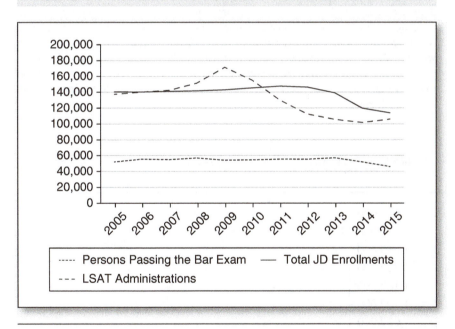

Sources: National Conference of Bar Examiners, "2015 Statistics," *The Bar Examiner* 85 (March 2016), accessed August 10, 2016, from www.ncbex.org/pdfviewer/?file=%2Fassets%2Fmedia_files%2FBar-Examiner%2Farticles%2F2016%2FBE-March2016-2015Statistics-Corrected103116.pdf; American Bar Association Section of Legal Education and Admission to the Bar, "Enrollment and Degrees Awarded, 1963–2012 Academic Years," accessed August 10, 2016, from www.americanbar.org/content/dam/aba/administrative/legal_education_and_admissions_to_the_bar/statistics/enrollment_degrees_awarded.authcheckdam.pdf; Law School Admission Council, "Total LSATs Administered—Counts and Percent Increases by Admin & Year," accessed August 10, 2016, from http://lsac.org/lsacresources/data/lsats-administered.

of law school matriculation in past years, the negative repercussions from the economy probably will not weaken the high demand for legal education. Approximately fifty thousand law graduates are admitted into the bar every year. As law professor Robin L. West explains, "Law schools provide an education in law, and there will always be a market, whether or not saturated, for well-educated lawyers." Even so, with a million-plus licensed attorneys in the United States, the competitive pressure to find employment is ever present and a reality for the bulk of law graduates entering into the legal marketplace (see Figure 4.2).[1]

The abundance of lawyers in the United States raises a number of issues that challenge the legal profession's structure and integrity. Critics and legal reformers are quick to observe that aspiring lawyers are often too preoccupied with the business of legal practice, a mind-set that is expressed through a hyperintensive obsession with getting into the most prestigious law schools and Big Law firms (discussed in this chapter's next section), since doing so is the best avenue for reaping the rewards of a lucrative legal career. What gets lost in the process, say detractors, is that the law is a profession and not a business at heart: while lawyers may be plentiful and making money is important, the real issue is that there are not enough solo and small firm lawyers who deliver legal services to consumers. The inequality in delivering legal services results in the profession being stratified into the haves and have-nots, which, in turn, translates into a lack of access to lawyers and courts. Reformers insist that the insularity and self-regulation of the legal profession, along with the stubbornness of law schools to change traditional pedagogies or doctrine-based degree programs to more flexible "practice ready" methods of law instruction in the twenty-first century, aggravate the resulting lack of access to the legal system for most citizens.[2]

Figure 4.2   Total Lawyer Population, 2005–2015

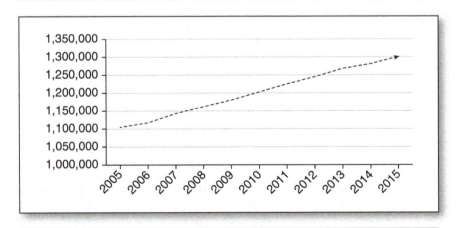

Source: American Bar Association, "ABA National Lawyer Population Survey," accessed August 10, 2016, from www.americanbar.org/content/dam/aba/administrative/market_research/national-lawyer-population-by-state-2016.authcheckdam.pdf.

While the next chapter addresses these concerns in more detail, the present discussion focuses on the type of employment law school graduates can expect to secure once they enter the labor market. After a brief explanation of the historical rise of the business orientation of the American legal profession, the narrative turns to understanding the significant place Big Law holds in elite law firm practice. Thereafter, other traditional, and mostly less elite, legal practice areas are outlined. The chapter concludes with an analysis of alternative careers for law degree holders in nonlegal practice areas that do not necessarily require bar passage.

THE BUSINESS OF LEGAL PRACTICE

The legal profession is highly decentralized and stratified in terms of its basic governance and administration. Multiple stakeholders and entities, such as the American Bar Association (ABA), national and state judiciaries, and state bars, determine its organization, structure, and autonomy. Apart from governance and administration issues, the delivery of legal services is dispersed into a variety of practice settings, ranging from solo practice and large law firm orientations, to government, private (corporate) sector, public interest, and academia segments, plus nontraditional or alternative legal occupations (JD holders employed in positions that do not require bar passage). Within these work spaces, what lawyers do in practice is fundamentally affected by the basic roles they play as advocates or advisers. Whereas advocates, or trial attorneys, typically engage in criminal or civil litigation that requires spending time in a courthouse, advisers, or transactional lawyers, have minimal exposure to courthouses and instead render legal advice to clients about personal or business dealings, such as drafting wills, purchasing real estate, or completing the documentation to create new corporations. For these reasons, litigators spend their workdays preparing their clients' cases for settlement or trial: they perform legal research, draft pleadings and motions, and attend court. On the other hand, transactional attorneys rarely go to court. Rather, they usually do in-office tasks such as drafting documents and meeting with, or talking to, clients and other lawyers on the phone. Regardless of the role they play, all lawyers to some degree practice law by counseling their clients and using the generic skills of negotiation, writing, advocacy, and problem solving.[3]

Due to competitive pressures inside the United States and across the globe, lawyers increasingly are cognizant of the need to deliver their wares across multiple jurisdictions in a cost-efficient format that is adept at using the sophisticated tools of informational technology to keep fees and costs down. In addition, what lawyers do in practice is specialized by what area of law they are in and what skill set is required to perform their jobs. Moreover, there is a growing geographical disparity between the ready availability of legal services in urban areas as opposed to rural locations, where they are relatively absent or difficult to find. Furthermore, although significant inroads have been made in terms of diversifying its membership, by and large the legal profession still remains homogeneous and elitist in nature.[4] The complexity of the contemporary legal profession is confirmed by the fact that it operates like a business instead of what some traditional or elder-statesmen observers wish it could be. For critics, the persistent preoccupation with the pursuit of profit and the adoption of business structures to deliver legal services in the legal marketplace degrades professional commitments to public service, political statesmanship, and justice.[5]

The evolution of the business of legal practice has its roots in the late nineteenth century, a time when legal education began to change and the country started to industrialize its economy in the aftermath of the Civil War and Reconstruction. The declining use of apprenticeships coincided with the formal institutionalization of university-based law school instruction and the widespread adoption of teaching doctrinal law through the casebook method (discussed in Chapter 3). Moving away from lecture as the usual form of classroom legal training is profitable because it caters to large class sizes, and sizable enrollment revenue, for law schools. During the same time period, influential local bar organizations in large cities collaborated with the American Bar Association (established in 1878) and a new private accreditation entity, the Association of American Law Schools (founded in 1900), to lobby state legislatures to enact restrictive law school entry and bar admission standards. In addition, the organized bar instituted a new code of ethical conduct, first introduced in 1908 as the Canons of Ethics, that reinforced the ability of lawyers to self-regulate all aspects of their ethical behavior in all of the states through their adoption of the Model Code of Professional Responsibility. As discussed in the next chapter, the combined effect of these transformations empowered the legal profession to insulate itself from outside competitive pressures under a unitary model that monopolized the control and access to legal services.[6]

The historical confluence of these events restricted access to the profession and legal goods while also putting lawyers in the unique position to establish what French sociologist Alexis de Tocqueville characterized as an "aristocracy of profession" that helped generate "a cartel of elite law firms that controlled the upper segment of the legal market through the first half of the twentieth century."[7] The growth of corporate wealth at the turn of the twentieth century supplied the backdrop for the rise of the so-called Wall Street law firm, the foundation for traditional law firm practice that prevailed until the mid-1960s. Thereafter, for a variety of reasons, the legal profession witnessed another transformation that led to the rise of what is popularly referred to as Big Law, an explosion of elite large law firms and megafirms that began to function differently from earlier large law firm practices. In part due to the 2008 economic downturn, Big Law's structure and practice norms are still evolving; but some legal observers are predicting Big Law's demise because its model for delivering legal services in the future is unsustainable in light of intensified global competition and a shifting, if not unreliable, client base.[8] The controversies surrounding Big Law's growth and its implications are discussed next.

BIG LAW AND ITS IMPACT ON THE LEGAL PROFESSION

In the late nineteenth and early twentieth centuries, corporate industrial leaders and entrepreneurial lawyers joined forces to build the foundation of elite large law firm practice. The Wall Street law firm, or traditional law firm model, emerged in the 1890s under the leadership of a New York City attorney, Paul D. Cravath, a cofounder of Cravath, Swaine & Moore. With the lessons learned while clerking in Walter Carter's law firm, Cravath strategically recruited the best talent from elite law schools in an effort to build a law practice with "anonymous organization men" who were "steadfastly loyal to the firm that had hired them fresh out of law school, moving only if the firm informed them it could not advance them to partnership." As an incentive to generate firm loyalty, the traditional model used an "up or out" promotion policy to cultivate the best lawyers while enhancing the firm's general reputation by building long-term relationships with corporate clients. Associates who did well advanced to partner, while less successful ones were asked to leave the firm, only to be replaced by new elite recruits. Associate attorneys were thus committed to the firm's collective well-being because it aligned with their promotion-to-partner aspirations—the price of moving forward was spending long hours at the law firm and tacitly agreeing to not make a lateral change to another firm in search of more lucrative employment opportunities. Although the environment resembled a sweatshop, a successful associate could reasonably expect to become a partner, and begin to share in the firm's profits with other partners (co-owners of the firm), within five to nine years.[9]

The Cravath traditional law firm model took root in several cities and later spread throughout the nation. It helped institutionalize a legal private practice setting that catered to well-resourced companies and favored the generation of stable corporate revenue, elements of practice that avoided the risks associated with unreliable or less-than-lucrative small business or individual client representation. Organizationally, the firm's growth relied on hiring and promotion decisions that preferred advancement from within; thus, partners and associates rarely came into or left the firm laterally from other industry or government practice milieus. As it evolved, the Wall Street firm model had a number of traits that gelled together nicely if the competition from other law firms and client demands remained at bay. Besides reinforcing specialization and commercialization, the traditional law firm's management practices reflect what some scholars call a "tournament" of norms and internal policies that centered on a well-defined organizational hierarchy and promotion-to-partner incentives.[10]

Under the traditional law firm model, the firm's tournament players are divided into two groups: (1) a legion of inexperienced associate attorneys hired straight from elite law schools or highly coveted judicial clerkships at a fixed annual salary and (2) fewer senior or experienced partners who are co-owners of the firm and share in the firm's profits. Whereas associates are obliged to remain loyal to the firm and work excruciatingly long hours in the hope of being promoted to partner after a probationary term of service, senior partners manage associates and use their experience to train them with the expectation of building a reputable firm and stable corporate client base.[11] While in tournament, initially firms billed clients through fixed rate schedules set by regional bar associations; but, later, underling associates charged for their time through billable hours (that often did not itemize expenses), a cost that was assumed by corporate clients, which, in turn, reinforced a business model that increased firm revenues and profit shares between partners. Having a high ratio of associates to partners was a key source of organizational leverage since having an army of associates and fewer partners reaped a greater yield of firm monies and partner profits. Corporate clients had little inclination to complain because they did not have enough information from firms to make informed choices about the scope and cost of representation; and, in part, they trusted the firms' partners through the development of long-standing relationships. Notably, the bulk of Cravath-inspired law firms were like the clients they served, so they lacked ethnic and religious diversity, a characteristic that persisted for most of the twentieth century.[12]

Organizational large elite law firm culture began to change in the 1960s and 1970s. Increasing global and domestic government regulation forced corporations to comply with new statutory and administrative mandates, so the demand for legal services grew in the areas of civil rights, employment, product liability, intellectual property, antitrust, securities, and contract law. The rising costs of meeting the demand led big business to look inward to see if in-house counsel could manage legal files and costs more efficiently instead of relying on expensive outside counsel in large law firms, as it had in the past. As a result, the competition among larger law firms intensified, the time to partnership lengthened or vanished for many associates, and lateral movements of partners and associates, once rare, began to proliferate in the 1970s. Also, a few large law firms began to move away from using fixed fee schedules by adopting a billable hour system in order to monitor and keep in check costs. After a Supreme Court ruling struck down fixed fees as an antitrust violation, the billable hour became the industry standard after 1975. Moreover, additional Supreme Court rulings, most notably *Bates v. State Bar of Arizona* (1977), eased bar-imposed restrictions on lawyer advertising. At the same time, an aggressive type of legal media coverage emerged from newspapers like the *National Law Journal* and *American Lawyer*, which began to publicize the size of law firms, their revenues, profit-per-partner metrics, client lists, and the starting salaries of lawyers, all topics that before then were shielded from public view.[13]

Amid these changes, competition within the industry deepened, forcing the ranks of associates to swell and causing entry-level salaries for top associates to rise sharply, thus increasing legal costs. In turn, the number of large elite firms skyrocketed. From 1960 to the mid-1980s, there was a twelvefold increase in law firms with more than fifty lawyers, from forty to over five hundred. The rising number of large law firms accelerated the growth of firm size and led to widespread geographical expansion. By 1988, nearly 1,200 lawyers were in the largest law firm, and over 150 firms were bigger than the largest law firm in 1968. In contrast to the norm in 1960 of having a single firm located in one city, by the 1980s law firms had rapidly established multiple branches in several urban locations. Over the same period, large law firms outpaced other segments of the legal profession in generating increased revenues and profitability, which caused their market share to double.[14]

The explosion of large elite law firms continued into the twenty-first century. Megafirms expanded their global reach by opening several international offices and creating a more diversified array of practice areas for clients interested in having a single law firm handle all of their legal needs in a "one-stop shop" format (see Table 4.1). The need for megafirms was fueled by mergers between large multinational companies because the conglomerates required legal services from law firms in different countries, which could handle an assortment of business-related practice areas, such as M&A (mergers and acquisitions) work and other corporate finance, tax, securities, environmental, employment, or antitrust law matters. Megafirms use their massive size and high-salaried associate attorney ranks, culled from elite law schools, to render specialized legal advice, supply litigation services (including extensive document preparation and review), and provide assistance in drafting administrative regulations and legislation, as well as performing lobbying activities. The growing importance of incorporating rapidly evolving Internet and digital technologies, along with fending off competition from other firms and

Table 4.1 Top Five Megafirms

Law Firm and Location	Practice Areas	Number Attorneys	Number Partners/ Associates	Starting Salaries Associates
Baker McKenzie (Chicago) www.bakermckenzie .com/en	Antitrust Banking Litigation Int'l Property Technology	4,245	1,421/2,942 # 702 (16%) ## 719 (16%)	$145,00 to $180,000
DLA Piper (New York) www.dlapiper.com/ en/us	Finance Int'l Property Litigation Real Estate Tax	3,756	1,223/2,306 # 386 (10%) ## 837 (22%)	$160,000
Norton Rose Fulbright (Houston) www.nortonroseful bright.com	Business Law Int'l Property Regulation Finance	3,461	1,175/1,835 # 912 (27%) ## 262 (8%)	$160,000 to $180,000
Jones Day (Washington) www.jonesday.com	Litigation Regulation Health Care Int'l Property	2,510	928/1,391 # 928 (36%) ## 0 (0%)	$160,000 to $180,000
Hogan Lovells (Washington) www.hoganlovells .com	Corp. Finance Regulation Litigation Int'l Property	2,101	805/1,711 # 533 (21%) ## 272 (11%)	$180,000

Sources: Internet Legal Research Group, "America's Largest 350 Law Firms" (Updated 2016), accessed August 17, 2016, from www.ilrg.com/nlj250/; Vault, "2017 Vault Law 100," accessed February 19, 2017, from www.vault.com/company-rankings/law/vault-law-100.

Notes: # Equity partners; ## Nonequity partners (percentages of each in parentheses).

low-cost legal providers that clients outsource their legal work to instead of large firms, has led megafirms to adjust their business models. As some legal scholars put it, the challenge of efficiently managing complex organizations has required large law firms "to adopt more of the business strategies and practices that are common in most other sectors."[15]

Over the past few decades, the competitive pressures of globalization, rapidly changing technological developments, and increasing client expectations impelled other changes in Big Law, which, in turn, significantly affected the legal profession. As their activities became more publicly transparent and business savvy, a number of elite law firms moved away from the traditional Cravath model by adopting a two-tiered partnership organization in order to increase profitability. In the traditional law firm model, partners shared profits equally, thus creating a "free rider" problem in which partners would rely on the revenue contributions of their colleagues by shirking their "rainmaking" (developing their client list, or book of business) obligations shortly after attaining partnership status. By contrast, a two-tiered law firm model diminishes the effects of free riding by making compensation merit based, a business reality that elevates rainmakers or business-producing lawyers to equity partners while relegating less valuable attorneys to nonequity partnership classifications. Sometimes ridiculed as glorified associates, nonequity partners typically perform the legal work generated by others; but they are adept at completing management or specialized project tasks that are essential to building the firm's brand and keeping the organization running smoothly. Still, while nonequity partners are paid a fixed salary, they do not reap the financial rewards that are linked to firm profitability. In addition, the two-tiered arrangement lessens the risk that rainmaking partners do not defect and make a lateral move to a competitor if they are dissatisfied with allowing less valuable colleagues to benefit from their book of business. Yet, while they stand to enjoy the profits of the firm's success, equity partners are forced to work harder due to the threat of being "de-equitized" or demoted to nonequity status in the event their performance slips. In spite of their strengths and weaknesses, by the mid-2000s many elite law firms had made the switch to two-tiered firms; and, by 2016, of the *National Law Journal* list of the five hundred largest firms, roughly 30 percent of full-time attorneys are equity partners.[16]

The emergence of two-tiered law firms removed seniority or age as a traditional metric of becoming an owner (and profit-sharing) attorney in the firm. Having a two-tiered business arrangement also intensified the pressure to gain, and sustain, equity partnership status by continuously remaining productive and bringing in clients; and it forced firms to keep productive partners in equity status to guard against the risk that they might leave the firm and take their clients with them. The professional advancement rules for nonpartner lawyers changed as well. In lieu of working toward partnership in the traditional up-or-out fashion, associates are put into different tracks. Under the contemporary two-tiered law firm model, associate attorneys who are deemed to have income- or business-producing potential are placed into a partnership track. All other associates work in the law firm in the non–partnership track. The two-track configuration fundamentally changes the nature and scope of professional advancement within Big Law firms.[17]

For partnership track associates, promotion to equity status is uncertain and rare, but possible. In contrast, like nonequity partners, non–partnership track associates are assigned into permanent employee status, but with fewer workload demands (analogous to receiving the security of academic tenure, or a guarantee of stable employment, at a fixed level of compensation). Further down the hierarchical pecking order are lawyers who are employed by the firm or who are hired to do legal tasks at a far cheaper rate than law firm associates. These include "of counsel" (typically, retired attorneys), staff attorneys, and contract attorneys, among others. To illustrate, a San Francisco, California–based law firm with over a thousand attorneys, Orrick, Herrington & Sutcliffe (Orrick), built an operations center in Wheeling, West Virginia, with three hundred employees as a cost-saving measure to deliver legal services; and, of those, a small subset are contract or staff attorneys who perform the rote tasks of what associate attorneys might do, such as completing boilerplate legal tasks or reviewing documents in preparation for trial.[18] Yet they are paid a wage that is typically half the salary of what associates earn who are working at the same firm. While career or staff attorneys have more long-term job security and are likely to receive benefits or possibly a promotion, contract attorneys might be paid by the hour (e.g., $20 an hour for document reviews) on a short-term basis, with greatly diminished opportunities to get benefits or promotions as part of their employment packages. For these reasons, some critics classify the lower-rung positions in the contemporary two-tiered law firm model as "second class," or "déclassé law firm jobs."[19]

Accordingly, instead of the traditional law firm "tournament" model, which incentivizes associates to achieve partnership status after a successful apprenticeship within the firm, the contemporary two-tiered structure of Big Law practice resembles what some characterize as an "elastic tournament" model; that is, it consists of "a firm in which a core of owner-partners is surrounded by a much larger mantle of employed lawyers that includes not only aspiring associates, but also non-equity partners, permanent associates, of-counsel and de-equitized former partners." Under the rules of the elastic tournament, the rewards that have been conventionally linked in the past to becoming a partner are now contingent on and more reminiscent of a perpetual journey that spans an attorney's career (to retirement or death), simply because there is always a risk of being de-equitized or forced to retirement status unless the partner is committed to working longer hours to earn his or her keep or retain his or her reputation within the firm.[20] Figure 4.3 is a visual depiction of what the contemporary two-tiered law firm structure might look like in relation to the traditional law firm model.

The resilience of Big Law's organizational and management practices was tested with the onset of the 2008 recession that witnessed the collapse of U.S. housing, banking, and capital markets. According to some estimates, by 2009 the top 250 large law firms lost 4 percent of their lawyers, and 15 of the top 75 firms were deprived of more than 100 lawyers each. Firm bankruptcies, layoffs, downsizing in staff, and slowdowns in new hiring reached new, unprecedented levels. Also, the economic downturn caused massive employment among new law school graduates and reductions in associate starting pay, and there was an exodus of partners and associates who sought better employment prospects by making lateral moves in the industry. Technological advancements and increased scrutiny of billing practices increasingly led clients to outsource legal services that were provided in-house or by other professionals (accountants, computer programmers, and the like) domestically or abroad or by nonlawyers because they could do boilerplate legal tasks, such as document preparation, inexpensively. In line with these trends, corporate clients turned to in-house counsel to do work that was once sent out to Big Law firms, and they began to insist that Big Law firms enter into "alternative fee arrangements," such as flat fees, instead of paying billable hour agreements. These changes, among others, caused some legal observers to proclaim the death or impending demise of Big Law, a fate that portended a radical if not irreversible structural change in the way legal services are delivered in the United States and abroad.[21]

Figure 4.3   Elite Large Law Firm Organization

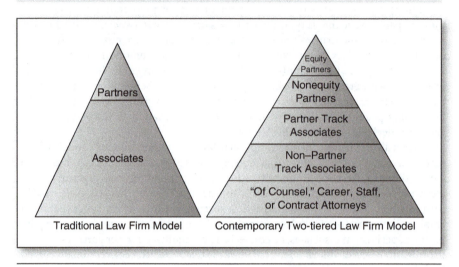

Source: Derived from Albert H. Yoon, "The Path of the Law: Evolution of the Legal Profession, 1955–2005," *Law School Admission Council, Grants Report 15-01* (October 2015), accessed August 16, 2016, from www.lsac.org/docs/default-source/research-(lsac-resources)/gr-15-01.pdf, 21.

While Big Law is likely to endure, law graduates seeking the lucrative rewards of becoming a part of it must be cognizant of the difficulties of landing a job in an elite large law firm and then, if successful, to survive in the demanding and high-pressure idiosyncrasies of its workplace. Among ABA-approved law schools, 15 percent (30 out of 206) supply most of the nation's Big Law firm employment (see Table 4.2). Only 30 law schools in the nation trained 76 percent of 500-plus and 59 percent of 250-plus Big Law positions. Further, employment data from the American Bar Association indicates that only 19 law schools, or 9 percent, of ABA-accredited law schools in the United States placed only one or two graduates in 250-plus or 500-plus Big Law firms.

Table 4.2 contains other notable information about Big Law recruiting and placement practices: (1) with the exception of Yale University and Stanford University, most Big Law employers hire from the top ten *U.S. News & World Report* (USNWR)–ranked law schools in the nation; (2) eight law schools in the USNWR top ten—New York University, Columbia University, University of Michigan, Harvard University, University of Virginia, University of Pennsylvania, University of Chicago, and University of California at Berkeley—supplied 243 graduates, or 23 percent, of employment to 250-plus firms and 1,329, or 33.2 percent, to 500-plus firms; (3) only a few of the top twenty-five USNWR-ranked schools—Georgetown University, George Washington University, Duke University, Northwestern University, University of California at Los Angeles, University of Texas at Austin, Cornell University, Emory University, Vanderbilt University, and University of Minnesota—provided 223 graduates, or 21 percent of employment, to 250-plus

Table 4.2   Big Law Employment, 2015

Rank	Law School	Total Number (250–500 Firms)	Total Number (500-Plus Firms)
1	New York University	46	258
2	Columbia University	44	253
3	Georgetown University	40	243
4	University of Michigan	34	217
5	Harvard University	31	161
6	University of Virginia	31	148
7	Fordham University	29	135
8	George Washington University	25	130
9	Duke University	24	109
10	Northwestern University	23	105
11	University of Pennsylvania	23	102
12	UCLA	23	100
13	University of Chicago	22	98
14	UC Berkeley	22	92
15	University of Texas at Austin	21	90
16	Cornell University	20	88
17	Boston College	18	85
18	Emory University	15	63
19	University of Washington	14	61
20	University of North Carolina	14	57
21	Tulane University	13	53
22	Vanderbilt University	12	48
23	University of Wisconsin	12	47
24	University of Minnesota	11	46

(Continued)

Table 4.2   (Continued)

Rank	Law School	Total Number (250–500 Firms)	Total Number (500-Plus Firms)
25	Yeshiva University (Cardozo)	10	45
26	Southern Methodist University	10	43
27	University of Illinois	10	42
28	University of Florida	10	42
29	Stetson University	10	36
30	University of Notre Dame	9	32
Total Number of 2014 Graduates That Top 30 Law Schools Placed in Big Law		626	3,029
Total Number and Percent of All 2014 Graduates Placed in Big Law Firms		1,059 (59.1%)	4,008 (75.6%)

Sources: American Bar Association, "Law School Employment Database," accessed August 13, 2016, from www.americanbar.org/groups/legal_education/resources/statistics.html. See also *U.S. News & World Report*, "Best Law Schools (Ranked in 2016)," accessed August 13, 2016, from http://grad-schools.usnews.rankingsandreviews.com/best-graduate-schools/top-law-schools/law-rankings?int=a1d108.

firms and 1,054 graduates, or 26.3 percent, to 500-plus firms; and (4) only the top twenty-five USNWR-ranked schools, or 12 percent of all ABA-accredited law schools, provided 44 percent of employment to 250-plus firms and 50 percent to 500-plus firms. Moreover, Boston College, University of Washington, University of Wisconsin, Fordham University, University of North Carolina, and Tulane University, which are top-fifty USNWR-ranked schools, delivered 100 graduates, or 9 percent, of employment to 250-plus firms and 438 graduates, or 11 percent, to 500-plus firms. Accordingly, only the top fifty USNWR-ranked law schools in the nation produce 21 percent of employment to 250-plus firms and 61 percent to 500-plus firms.

Finally, only the University of Illinois (#40, USNWR), University of Florida (#48, USNWR), and Yeshiva University (Cardozo, #74, USNWR) are in the top one hundred USNWR-ranked law schools that successfully placed their graduates in Big Law: only 30, or 3 percent, were hired into 250-plus firms, and 129, or 3 percent, into 500-plus firms. Notably, the lowest USNWR-ranked school in the top thirty Big Law employment list in Table 4.2, Stetson University (#103, USNWR), was responsible for placing 10, or less than 1 percent, in 250-plus firms and only 36 graduates, or less than 1 percent, in 500-plus firms. As one legal scholar put it, these statistics indicate that "[f]or the majority of law graduates, landing a big law firm job is a mirage."[22]

Students interested in working in Big Law also must be aware of the assets and liabilities of practicing law as a new associate attorney in a large law firm. Often recruited in the summer before their graduation, law graduates join Big Law firms at starting salaries that range from $160,000 to $180,000, plus performance bonuses. While some firms, in difficult economic times or for other reasons, might use merit-based bonus formulas, in robust economies a lockstep raise is given to all associates for every year spent at the firm. In 2016, at New York's Cravath, Swaine & Moore, summer associates were paid $3,500 per week; and, once associates were hired, first-year base salaries began at $180,000 and then rose incrementally (second year, $190,000; third year, $210,000; fourth year, $235,000; fifth year, $260,000; sixth year, $280,000; and seventh year, $315,000). Significantly, the amount of bonuses that are given may be tied to reaching or exceeding a threshold number of billing hours per year; and some, but not all, firms credit *pro bono* work (volunteer, unpaid legal services) toward meeting the threshold. If the minimum number is met, the year-end bonus payments can be quite substantial, ranging from $10,000 in the first year to $50,000 in the sixth, or more.[23]

Still, new associates are expected to log at least 2,000 billable hours per year, and it is not uncommon to record 2,400 or more, which leaves little time to do anything outside of work; and, at least in the first years, most of it is spent doing massive and mind-numbing document reviews (of millions of print and digital documents given by clients or opposing counsel in preparing for trials) for 8 to 12 hours a day, over several successive weeks or months at a time. While associates gain more responsibilities over time, they often do so without any meaningful mentorship or constructive feedback by senior associates or partners, in part due to the firm's massive size and the impersonal nature of the hierarchical organization. Not surprisingly, under these working conditions, and since the traditional law firm model is long gone and "the likelihood of making partner at the firm joined right out of law school is close to zero," many newly hired Big Law associates choose to leave the firm after a few years for better employment opportunities.[24]

PRIVATE PRACTICE AND OTHER LEGAL EMPLOYMENT SETTINGS

The 2008 Great Recession impacted elite graduates and practitioners who became nervous about declining profitability and whether they would be able to hold on to their reputational prestige. It also created new worries for the majority of lawyers who work in other practice settings and oftentimes find it difficult to thrive professionally. The legal profession confronted similar economic distress in the past in the Depression era and early New Deal period. While it is difficult to know if the profession is in the midst of any long-term structural change, the recession's impact underscores that the "challenges facing large law firms have come to resemble the challenges facing the blue collar bar, with the former confronted with experiencing not only status anxiety but also, like the rest of the profession, survival anxiety."[25] With few exceptions, the stratification of the legal profession into the elites and non-elites is an important and consistent theme that runs throughout any assessment of legal employment trends and opportunities. The ensuing discussion will address the realties and challenges of working in legal practice settings in smaller law firms, solo practice, business and industry, government, public interest, and legal academia. In the last section, alternative employment in nonlegal settings is discussed.

Private Practice

The American Bar Association reports that private practice is the most popular legal employment setting for lawyers since the 1980s. Among these lawyers, over 70 percent work in law firms of various sizes or solo practice. Whether lawyers decide to practice law in firms or go it alone is contingent on prevalent economic conditions and the reality of being able to land a job that requires bar passage immediately after law school.[26] In 2005, almost 50 percent of all U.S. lawyers were solo practitioners. Other lawyers toiled in small law firms of two to five lawyers (14 percent); small to medium-sized firms ranging from six to one hundred lawyers (22 percent); or large law firms of over one hundred attorneys (16 percent). As a subset of the aggregate demographics of the legal profession, research from the National Association for Law Placement (NALP) indicates that a majority of 2015 law graduates (51 percent) found employment in private practice, and 93 percent of those jobs required bar passage. In the 2015 class, a significant percentage found work in small law firms of twenty-five lawyers or fewer (nearly 50 percent) or in Big Law firms of five hundred or more attorneys (23 percent). While roughly 23 percent were employed in firms with over twenty-five to fewer than five hundred lawyers, only 3 percent of 2015 graduates opened solo practices.[27]

Amid the diversity of law firm practice, a large percentage (83 percent) of 2015 law graduates worked as associate attorneys in law firms, while considerably fewer grads (9 percent) were employed as law clerks. Six percent were hired as staff lawyers, and the remainder were paralegals or held administrative positions. While 2015 graduates reported that they earn salaries between $60,000 and $160,000 (in the 25th to 75th percentiles), law clerks, staff attorneys, paralegals, and other administrative positions were paid substantially less. Regardless of their position, attorneys are exposed to a wide variety of practice areas, such as trusts and estates, corporation, immigration, real estate, intellectual property, criminal, and tax law, among others. Many solo practitioners and small firms, especially in rural areas, represent individual clients, predominantly in criminal or civil cases addressing family law, personal injury lawsuits, real estate transactions, or probate law that require creating estate plans. Lawyers in bigger firms tend to cater to business clientele in commercial transactions that specialize in certain areas like tax or antitrust law.[28]

The bulk of law graduates do not work in Big Law. As a result, lawyers who do not (or cannot, because they are from nonelite schools) follow that career path and wish to engage in private practice are faced with the competitive challenges of finding sustainable legal work, especially in tight legal marketplace economies. As the NALP 2015 legal employment figures document, close to 12 percent of new grads did not find, or were still seeking, work; and, of those who were employed, almost 20 percent were looking for another job. Among the successful job seekers, many landed in small law firms with twenty-five lawyers or fewer but, more infrequently, immediately practiced law as solo practitioners.[29]

In part because of the 2008 recession's impact, lawyers engaged in small law firm and solo practice thus have begun to explore alternative ways to make a living and service their clientele. Styled "indie lawyering" and "disruptive innovation" methods of law practice, lawyers render legal advice and solve client problems by the innovative use of new technologies that promise to deliver low-cost but highly efficient legal services to cost-conscious clients and communities, an approach that threatens to "disrupt" or challenge established competitors and legal marketplace practices from the bottom up. Indie lawyering is an independent and individualized approach to law practice that some legal experts claim is becoming increasingly entrenched in urban and rural law practice. Using social media and Internet-based platforms such as email, texting, mobile apps, and Skype, practitioners design their law offices with flexible work schedules and locations (from their homes or in other companies directly on site) without expensive overhead. The availability of new technologies allows indie lawyers to tailor their legal commodities as craft, or customized, legal commodities that can be consumed and shared by clients or local communities that often cannot have their transactional legal needs met from cookie-cutter "big box" or mass-production Big Law firms or analogous legal outsourcing companies (e.g., litigating small claims disputes, preparing medical directives, or preparing contracts, leases, or wills, in either Big Law firms or other outlets such as LegalZoom, Shake, or Rocket Lawyer).[30]

By taking advantage of cutting-edge computer digital technologies, machine learning, and software programs, entrepreneurial lawyers in small firms or solo practices can supply their wares to clientele, such as local school boards, tenant associations, or individual consumers, which may not be able to afford the high cost of legal services. Legal scholars have identified several "new models of legal practice" that adopt groundbreaking technologies, such as opening "virtual law firms" or creating "innovative law firms and companies," that are the antithesis to Big Law practices since they strive to connect practitioners to consumers who traditionally cannot get their legal services from large law firms due to high cost and institutional barriers that deny access to courts. Thus, they may be increasingly attractive to practitioners who are sensitive to providing niche legal services to the hidden, or latent, legal marketplace (for consumers such as *pro se*, or unrepresented, litigants) or who wish to make their law practice more flexible and less dependent on meeting high-pressure rainmaking and billing practices that prevent lawyers from striking a reasonable work–life balance.[31] The work space challenges of successfully maintaining a sustainable and professionally sound law practice are addressed in further detail in the next chapter.

Business and Industry Law Practice

Research from the American Bar Association, the National Association for Law Placement, and empirical legal studies shows that a growing percentage of lawyers and law graduates are working in business and industry positions. In 2005, the ABA reported that 8 percent of lawyers were employed in private industry; but, by 2015, the percentage had risen to 15 percent among new graduates. The NALP survey of the 2015 class registered similar findings and data (17 percent), and the rate of attorneys employed in business and industry has steadily risen since the early 1990s. Notably, lawyers in this sector are paid a yearly salary between $55,000 and $89,500 (in the 25th to 75th percentile), and roughly a quarter of private industry jobs require bar passage.[32]

Law graduates in business and industry jobs work for a diverse array of private sector employers, including insurance companies, financial institutions, and accounting firms, among others. The Association of Corporate Counsel identifies that lawyers in this sector engage in a wide variety of business-related practice areas, such as litigation, real estate, technology, contracts, corporate securities, labor law and employment, energy and public utilities, intellectual property, and environmental law. While newly licensed lawyers ordinarily work in business or other legal settings for a number of years before being hired by a major corporation, an attractive and lucrative employment option for experienced attorneys is assuming the role of in-house, or general, counsel in Fortune 500 business organizations, including Apple, General Motors, General Electric, AT&T, JPMorgan Chase & Company, and others.[33]

In-house counsel perform legal services for only one client—the corporation or business entity for which they work. In that role, they provide legal advice on general business matters, along with negotiating deals, writing contracts, and cultivating corporate opportunities while pursuing strategies that avoid legal liabilities and minimize business risks. From a broader perspective, the significance of in-house counsel has grown in recent years since many legal experts question whether the predominant business model within the legal profession—namely, working in a large law firm—is economically viable in the aftermath of the 2008 recession. From this perspective, the prestige and importance of working as in-house counsel has grown since these professionals are now widely regarded as front-line actors who not only protect corporate legal interests but also play the role of being significant "gatekeepers for companies' outsourcing of work to law firms," a vital concern to business organizations that are keenly committed to reducing legal costs and expenses. Moreover, with an estimated sixty-five thousand in-house counsel working in the U.S. business industry, many reap large financial and professional rewards, with 22 percent earning more than $300,000 in salaries, bonus compensation, and other perks. One survey reports that the base pay for general counsel is over $600,000, and if other bonuses and perks are considered, many others earn compensation packages that exceed a million dollars. Another report from 2015 shows that the average salary for the top one hundred general counsel is more than $700,000, with numerous additional bonus and stock option compensation opportunities.[34]

At the same time, however, the once common perception among legal professionals that working in-house is a "professional haven" that offers a desirable combination of status, pay, and work–life balance is probably overstated. While some critics concede that in-house positions are more flexible and sensitive to the goals of increasing gender diversity and equality among peers, they also observe that the realities of the workplace reveal an underbelly of gender underrepresentation and inequality in senior powerful positions and that corporate legal employment has many of the same stressors that are linked to professional advancement that are found in Big Law firms. As one legal research study concludes, "The beliefs that in-house departments offer an attractive work–life balance and greater equality in promotion to positions of power and influence are exaggerated myths."[35]

Government, Public Interest Attorneys, and Legal Academia Positions

A relatively small percentage of law graduates seeking employment work for the federal, state, or local government. What lawyers do in government positions varies in accordance with whether they are connected to the legislative, executive, or judicial departments. Typically, such jobs include working as prosecutors, public defenders, or administrative, executive, or legislative staff. Almost thirty-six thousand attorneys, for example, work in federal agencies. Roughly 27 percent are found in the Department of Justice; 15 percent are in Treasury, Homeland Security, and Army; and the balance are spread across a multitude of other agencies. To be sure, a large percentage of government lawyers work in nonfederal capacities. Government lawyers, moreover, are committed to defending their respective governments' interests in a wide range of legal matters affecting criminal or civil litigation and, in general, enforce the law on behalf of public officials or give them advice on regulatory issues.[36] Even so, it is not usual for government lawyers to move laterally into the private sector after gaining valuable knowledge and experience in the public sector.[37]

Data from the American Bar Association and National Association for Law Placement indicate that 12 percent of 2015 graduates were hired by the government, and another 10 percent worked as judicial law clerks. Whereas a majority of government positions (73 percent) require bar passage, virtually all judiciaries on the federal, state, and local levels mandate that their law clerks have a law license. Generally, while federal judicial law clerks earn more money than their state or local counterparts, the starting salaries for clerkship positions range from $37,000 to $64,000 (in the 25th to 75th percentiles). As law clerks, attorneys typically are hired for shorter terms of service (one to three years), though some obtain permanent employment as staff or central lawyers working for the court. In performing their jobs, law clerks do legal research and help judges write internal memoranda, judicial orders, and judicial opinions. Notably, another perk to being hired as a law clerk is that it often opens the door for making a lateral move to either a Big Law position or a job as a law professor in the legal academy.[38]

Likewise, a small proportion of new 2015 law graduates found work in the public interest field (7 percent), and even fewer (2 percent) entered the legal academy in educational positions. While most public interest employment (77 percent) mandates passing the bar, it is not always necessary to enter the educational workforce. Indeed, most law professors do not actively practice law even though they may have passed the bar exam.[39] Regardless, with respect to public interest work, most attorneys are policy advocates for a variety of private concerns and public interest law firms. Often referred to as "public interest law organizations" or PILOs, or "cause lawyering," attorneys in this line of work supply legal services to the economically or politically downtrodden in order to give them access to the courts, simply because they cannot afford to hire private counsel. Among their range of duties, PILOs and cause lawyers give legal aid to individuals or the community as a whole; and, increasingly, they spend their professional time litigating significant and controversial issues of social and public policy reform. Many public interest lawyers, though, are paid substantially less than lawyers in other legal employment sectors: the NALP reports that 2015 graduates earn a salary between $41,300 and $55,000 (in the 25th to 75th percentiles).[40] Not surprisingly, then, studies have confirmed that graduates interested in pursuing public interest careers are fearful to do so due to low salaries and high student loan debt.[41] In response, many law schools offer some enticements to enter into public service through loan forgiveness or debt reduction programs.[42]

In contrast, lawyers who represent the legal academy work as law professors or assume administrative positions, such as career advisers, admissions personnel, or university counsel. Roughly one thousand applicants vie for tenure-track law professor positions in the United States every year, either formally through a recruitment process run by the Association of American Law Schools or informally by direct application to law schools. A growing trend is that applicants have an advanced degree (a master's or a doctorate) in another discipline or a higher-level degree in law such as an LLM (a one-year graduate degree that is earned after the three-year law degree). As in many facets of the legal profession, the competition to be hired as a law professor is especially keen, and some empirical studies report that only one in seven applicants is offered a tenure-track position among some two hundred ABA-accredited law schools in the United States.[43] Although NALP reports indicate that 2015 graduates in academic jobs earn between $41,250 and $60,000, a survey of 2015–2016 salaries shows that a large proportion of faculty across all regions of the country earn $100,000 or more per year at the pretenure assistant or associate rank level, excluding several thousand dollars in compensation as a summer stipend for research and other scholarly activities. Tenured professors at the associate and full professor rank earn substantially more, with many in the $150,000 to $190,000 range. Consequently, many law professors who are fortunate enough to get hired into legal academia enjoy significant professional autonomy and job security in performing teaching and legal research roles, which probably offsets the lower income that they might otherwise make in the private sector, especially if they are from elite law schools.[44]

ALTERNATIVE CAREERS: NONLEGAL JOBS

Many legal experts and commentators agree that economic pressures and new advancements in Internet and digital technologies have increased job competition for lawyers within the United States and abroad. For legal scholar Herbert Kritzer, the contemporary legal marketplace has moved in the direction of establishing a "postprofessional" era: that is, several factors have combined to let specialized nonlegal professionals do the work that traditionally was exclusively performed by licensed lawyers.[45] With the exception of secretarial and support staff, Kritzer argues that employment within the profession in the future will revolve around three broad types of "law workers" who are not necessarily competent to practice law but who can supply a broad array of legal services to clients. Law workers consist of "all individuals who deliver services of a legal nature," which may include rendering acutely specialized work, like tax preparation, tax law consulting, workers' compensation, or legal document preparation or, in the advocacy realm, legal assistants, paralegals, and alternative dispute resolution mediators who are autonomous in performing their jobs but most likely require licensed lawyer supervision. Similarly, the gains made in information technology have created opportunities for lawyers to become legal information engineers, legal consultants, or legal processors.[46]

Law graduates may enter into these and analogous positions simply by graduating from law school without having to pass the bar. Not being professionally licensed affords more flexibility to job seekers than seeking to find a niche in the legal marketplace that lets graduates (or even already employed lawyers) use their law degree in an alternative, or nonlegal, setting. Moreover, law students who pass the bar, or licensed lawyers who have been in the workforce, also may opt to forego traditional legal practice and enter into a law-related field that permits them to take advantage of their professional expertise. Law training facilitates graduates or licensed lawyers to work in the nonprofit and education sectors, the federal or state government, or the real estate or financial markets as Realtors or investment bankers.[47] Notably, the narrowing market for legal jobs has put the onus on law schools to prepare their students for alternative careers. While not uniformly done, many law schools have responded by increasingly offering "practice ready" courses in law and entrepreneurship, or both. Not surprisingly, the National Association for Law Placement reports that the number of recent law graduates entering directly into business or industry careers jumped from less than 8 percent in the early 1990s to 18 percent in recent years.[48]

The fact that a law degree may open nontraditional doors outside of the legal profession is confirmed by data showing that 2015 law graduates are moving into what the American Bar Association and the National Association for Law Placement refer to as "JD Advantage" jobs. According to the NALP, a full- or part-time JD Advantage job represents the "category of jobs for which bar passage is not required but for which a JD degree provides a distinct advantage."[49] In its 2017 Employment Questionnaire, the ABA identifies several types of positions as JD Advantage jobs, including corporate contract administrators, alternative dispute resolution specialists, government regulatory analysts, FBI agents, accountants, human resource or personnel employees, legal consultants, legal compliance specialists, educational admissions or career services officers, and employees working in law firm professional development. Although the ABA states that a JD Advantage job cannot earn that designation if a "JD is uncommon among persons holding such a position," the type of employment that falls within this category is broad in scope: it includes doctors or nurses who anticipate working in litigation, insurance, or risk management realms, as well as journalists and teachers (in higher education) and positions that are funded by law schools or universities either directly or by grant monies.[50] Similarly, the NALP lists a number of occupations ranging across academia, business and industry, government, private practice, and public interest settings, including law school research assistant or fellow, legal temporary agency work, accounting, management consulting, state or federal legislative or executive positions, law clerks or paralegals, and employees in public interest organizations. Students entering into the workforce in JD Advantage jobs can expect to earn salaries between $45,000 and $75,000.[51]

In its "Class of 2015 National Summary Report," the NALP indicates that 15 percent of law graduates identified themselves as having JD Advantage jobs, and most were full-time (15 percent) as opposed to part-time (2 percent). Of those positions, most JD Advantage employment was in the academic, business, government, and public interest settings. Predictably, far fewer JD positions were in private practice employment, simply because a large majority of that work requires bar passage.[52] Predictably, the percentage of law graduates assuming JD Advantage jobs increases as bar passage rates fall and unemployment grows in the legal marketplace. In 2013, 13 percent of graduates fell into this category, which, at the time, represented an all-time high since the NALP began to report analogous employment trends (using "Law Preferred" jobs as the operative category) in 2001.[53]

The definitions that the ABA and NALP use to classify JD Advantage jobs and employment trends have been subject to the criticism that they are too vague or substantively meaningless. Law professor Matt Leichter, for one, observes that some of the JD Advantage jobs, such as law clerk, paralegal, law school research fellow, and other undefined positions in business, are the type of employment that inherently underutilizes the skills that are developed by earning a law degree. In Leichter's estimation, JD Advantage jobs should be defined as those requiring professional judgment since his research claims that under the NALP criteria a much higher proportion of 2011 graduates, or 44 percent, held positions that did not take full advantage of the law degree. Furthermore, additional empirical studies report findings that show that lawyers in JD Advantage jobs are generally less satisfied in their work and almost half of the 2010 class was looking for another job nine months after graduation. At least for one legal expert, the research suggests that "[t]he most rational use of a law degree, at least during the early years of a career, is to practice law," and "if students want an intellectually challenging graduate program that prepares them for diverse careers, including ones that are law-related, today's universities offer many options: master's degrees in business, public affairs, public health, computer science, environmental engineering, and data analytics are just some of the opportunities." While there is room for disagreement on the issue, it is always advantageous for law students to explore a full range of their career options either before or while in law school, including the possibility of earning a joint degree, such as a JD/MBA (or similar degrees), to increase their chances of finding sustainable employment in a highly competitive legal or private sector marketplace.[54]

CONCLUSION

Students contemplating a legal career must understand the realities of legal education and the job market well before they enter and graduate from law school. While estimates vary, a legal scholar's survey of employment statistics from the legal profession indicates that more than a third of law graduates have not been able to find a full-time position in recent years. Moreover, only 65 percent of lawyers who found employment hold positions that require (or recommend) a law degree, and increasingly, graduates are finding work that does not mandate bar passage. Although there are some signs of improvement in the legal marketplace, as this chapter has shown, these employment trends are manifested by the most recent data reported from the ABA and the NALP. It is not surprising, then, that law professor Robin L. West concludes that "[b]oth the overall employment and the numbers in law firms are at new lows, whereas the numbers of graduates at nonprofits with their salaries or stipends paid by the schools, or working part time, in temporary positions, or in 'business,' are at new highs." In addition, she observes that not being able to find work is particularly disheartening in light of the fact that many students are forced to struggle to find employment after accumulating between $100,000 and $200,000 in student loan debt, or more.[55] Although it remains unclear how long these employment trends will persist, the impact of the 2008 recession and the vagaries of the legal marketplace have renewed calls for reforming the legal profession, a topic that is taken up in more detail in the next chapter.

SELECTED READINGS

Galanter, Marc, and William Henderson. "The Elastic Tournament: A Second Transformation of the Big Law Firm." *Stanford Law Review* 60 (2008): 1867–1929.

Galanter, Marc, and Thomas Palay. *Tournament of Lawyers: The Transformation of the Big Law Firm*. Chicago, Ill.: University of Chicago Press, 1991.

Impellizzeri, Amy. *Lawyer Interrupted: Successfully Transitioning from the Practice of Law—and Back Again*. Chicago, Ill.: American Bar Association, 2015.

Johnson, Creola. *Is a Law Degree Still Worth the Price? It Depends on What the Law School Has to Offer*. Durham, N.C.: Carolina Academic Press, 2014.

Kim, Jasper. *24 Hours with 24 Lawyers: Profiles of Traditional and Non-traditional Careers*. Eagan, Minn.: Aspatore, 2011.

Kritzer, Herbert M. *Lawyers at Work*. New Orleans, La.: Quid Pro Books, 2015.

Powell, Sarah. *BIGLAW: How to Survive the First Two Years of Practice in a Mega-Firm, or, the Art of Doc Review*. Durham, N.C.: Carolina Academic Press, 2013.

Swaine, Robert T. *The Cravath Firm and Its Predecessors: 1819–1947*. New York, N.Y.: Ad Press, 1948.

WEB LINKS

American Bar Association, "Legal Career Central" (www.abalcc.org)

Bureau of Labor Statistics, "Occupational Outlook Handbook: Legal Occupations" (www.bls .gov/ooh/legal/home.htm)

FindLaw, "Law Career Center" (http://careers.findlaw.com)

National Association for Law Placement (www.nalp.org)

National Association for Law Placement Alternative Career Committee, "Alternative Careers for Lawyers: Web Sites of Interest" (www.nalp.org/uploads/AltCareersWebsites_ rev2010.pdf)

ENDNOTES

1. Recent bar passage rates, law school matriculation trends, and total lawyer population numbers are reported in National Conference of Bar Examiners, "2015 Statistics," *The Bar Examiner* 85 (March 2016): 16; American Bar Association Section of Legal Education and Admissions to the Bar, "Enrollment and Degrees Awarded, 1963–2012 Academic Years," accessed July 26, 2016, from www.americanbar.org/content/dam/aba/administrative/ legal_education_and_admissions_to_the_bar/statistics/enrollment_degrees_awarded .authcheckdam.pdf; and American Bar Association, "ABA National Lawyer Population Survey: Historical Trend in Total National Lawyer Population, 1878–2016," accessed July 26, 2016, from www.americanbar.org/content/dam/aba/administrative/market_ research/total-national-lawyer-population-1878-2016.authcheckdam.pdf. See also Robin L. West, *Teaching Law: Justice, Politics, and the Demands of Professionalism* (New York, N.Y.: Cambridge University Press, 2014), 20.

2. Analyses of the effects of the legal system's elitism on creating wealth disparities in litiga- tion and legal professional stratification are found in Marc Galanter, "Why the 'Haves' Come Out Ahead: Speculations on the Limits of Legal Change," *Law and Society Review* 9 (1974): 95–160; and John P. Heinz, Robert L. Nelson, Rebecca L. Sandefur, and Edward O. Laumann, *Urban Lawyers: The New Social Structure of the Bar* (Chicago, Ill.: University of Chicago Press, 2005). Criticisms and proposals to reform the legal profession are found in Deborah L. Rhode, *The Trouble with Lawyers*

(New York, N.Y.: Oxford University Press, 2015); Benjamin H. Barton, *Glass Half Full: The Decline and Rebirth of the Legal Profession* (New York, N.Y.: Oxford University Press, 2015); William Domnarski, *Swimming in Deep Water: Lawyers, Judges, and Our Troubled Legal Profession* (Chicago, Ill.: American Bar Association, 2014); Creola Johnson, *Is a Law Degree Still Worth the Price? It Depends on What the Law School Has to Offer* (Durham, N.C.: Carolina Academic Press, 2014); Steven J. Harper, *The Lawyer Bubble* (New York, N.Y.: Basic Books, 2013); James E. Moliterno, *The American Legal Profession in Crisis: Resistance and Responses to Change* (New York, N.Y.: Oxford University Press, 2010); Thomas D. Morgan, *The Vanishing Lawyer* (New York, N.Y.: Oxford University Press, 2010); Douglas Litowitz, *The Destruction of Young Lawyers: Beyond One L* (Akron, Ohio: University of Akron Press, 2006); and Anthony Kronman, *The Lost Lawyer: Failing Ideals of the Legal Profession* (Cambridge, Mass.: Belknap Press of Harvard University Press, 1993).

3.   National Association for Law Placement, "Prelaw—What Do Lawyers Do?," accessed September 2, 2016, from www.nalp.org/what_do_lawyers_do.

4.   See, e.g., Christopher P. Banks and David M. O'Brien, *The Judicial Process: Law, Courts, and Judicial Politics* (Thousand Oaks, Calif.: Sage/CQ Press, 2015), 121–125 (detailing the lack of diversity in the judiciary, especially in Tables 4.2 and 4.3).

5.   These themes are discussed in Rhode, *Trouble with Lawyers*; and Kronman, *Lost Lawyer*. General descriptions of the contemporary nature of the legal profession are found in Herbert M. Kritzer, *Lawyers at Work* (New Orleans, La.: Quid Pro Books, 2015), 287–318; and Albert H. Yoon, "The Path of the Law: Evolution of the Legal Profession, 1955–2005," *Law School Admission Council Grants Report 15–01* (October 2015), accessed August 15, 2016, from http://lsac.org/docs/default-source/research-(lsac-resources)/gr-15-01.pdf, 4.

6.   Dana A. Remus, "Out of Practice: The Twenty-first-Century Legal Profession," *Duke Law Journal* 63 (2014): 1243, 1248–1252. See also Banks and O'Brien, *Judicial Process*, 142–145.

7.   As quoted in Andrew Bruck and Andrew Canter, "Supply, Demand, and the Changing Economics of Large Law Firms," *Stanford Law Review* 60 (2008): 2087, 2092.

8.   See, e.g., Larry E. Ribstein, "The Death of Big Law," *Wisconsin Law Review* 2010 (2010): 749–815. Ribstein posits that Big Law's problems may only be solved by using a different business model that incorporates ownership of firm property that is attractive to outside financing. Ibid., 752.

9.   Ribstein, "Death of Big Law," 756–757; Bemard A. Burk and David McGowan, "Big but Brittle: Economic Perspectives on the Future of the Law Firm in the New Economy," *Columbia Business Law Review* 2011 (2011): 1, 8; William D. Henderson, "Three Generations of U.S. Lawyers: Generalist, Specialists, Project Managers," *Maryland Law Review* 70 (2011): 373, 375; Wayne K. Hobson, "Symbol of the New Profession: Emergence of the Large Law Firm, 1870–1915," in *The New High Priests: Lawyers in Post–Civil War America*, ed. Gerard W. Gawalt (Westport, Conn.: Greenwood Press, 1984), 19–20; and Robert T. Swaine, *The Cravath Firm and Its Predecessors: 1819–1947* (New York, N.Y.: Ad Press, 1948).

10. Marc Galanter and Thomas Palay, *Tournament of Lawyers: The Transformation of the Big Law Firm* (Chicago, Ill.: University of Chicago Press, 1991). See also Burk and McGowan, "Big but Brittle," 8–11.

11. One legal scholar emphasizes that the standard economic model of law firms originates in the firm's overriding interest in bonding its lawyers to a commitment to build a strong firm reputation. Ribstein, "Death of Big Law," 753–757.

12. Bruck and Canter, "Supply, Demand, and the Changing Economics of Large Law Firms," 2092–2095. See also Ribstein, "Death of Big Law," 756–757.

13. Bruck and Canter, "Supply, Demand, and the Changing Economics of Large Law Firms," 2093–2096; Burk and McGowan, "Big but Brittle," 14–20. See also *Goldfarb v. Virginia*

State Bar, 421 U.S. 773 (1975), and *Bates v. State Bar of Arizona*, 433 U.S. 350 (1977), which ended mandatory bar-imposed minimum fee schedules and struck down a state ban on lawyer advertising.

14. Burk and McGowan, "Big but Brittle," 12–15, 19–23; Bruck and Canter, "Supply, Demand, and the Changing Economics of Large Law Firms," 2093–2096.

15. Carolyn B. Lamm and Hugh Verrier, "Large Law Firms: A Business Model, a Service Ethic," in *The Relevant Lawyer: Reimagining the Future of the Legal Profession*, ed. Paul A. Haskins (Chicago, Ill.: ABA Standing Committee on Professionalism, Center for Professional Responsibility, 2015), 103–112. See also Randall S. Thomas, Stewart J. Schwab, and Robert G. Hansen, "Megafirms," *North Carolina Law Review* 80 (2001): 115–197.

16. Katelyn Polantz, "An Army of Attorneys: Total Head Count at the Nation's 350 Largest Law Firms Dipped Only Fractionally Last Year," *American Lawyer* 38, no. 8 (August 1, 2016). See also Marc Galanter and William Henderson, "The Elastic Tournament: A Second Transformation of the Big Law Firm," *Stanford Law Review* 60 (2008): 1867, 1873–1876, 1892.

17. The different titles, roles, and performance obligations of equity versus nonequity partners are discussed in William D. Henderson, "An Empirical Study of Single-Tier Versus Two-Tier Partnerships in the Am Law 200," *North Carolina Law Review* 84 (2006): 1691, 1707–1711.

18. Whereas staff attorneys are permanent employees of the law firm, contract attorneys are not firm employees. Instead, contract attorneys are contracted with external vendors and outside legal staffing companies, such as Robert Half Legal. Big Law firms may use one or the other, or both; typically to do document reviews; and their billing rates are far less (i.e., say, $180 an hour) than associate billing rates (i.e., $350 an hour). If both are used in a document review, contract attorneys do the first review of millions of documents gathered from a client, and staff attorneys do a second review by coding them with more sophisticated legal analysis. Associate attorneys then supervise and manage the staff attorneys and their work product. Sarah Powell, *BIGLAW: How to Survive the First Two Years of Practice in a Mega-Firm, or, the Art of Doc Review* (Durham, N.C.: Carolina Academic Press, 2013), 39.

19. Johnson, *Is a Law Degree Still Worth the Price?*, 175–179.

20. The quote is from Galanter and Henderson, "Elastic Tournament," 1877. See also ibid., 1873–1882; George P. Baker and Rachel Parkin, "The Changing Nature of the Legal Services Industry and the Careers of Lawyers," *North Carolina Law Review* 84 (2006): 1635–1641 (n. 11).

21. See Ribstein, "Death of Big Law," 749–815; Stephen M. Sheppard, "The American Legal Profession in the Twenty-first Century," *American Journal of Comparative Law* 62 (2014): 241–272; and Eli Wald, "The Great Recession and the Legal Profession," *Fordham Law Review* 78 (2010): 2051–2066.

22. Johnson, *Is a Law Degree Still Worth the Price?*, 186.

23. Vault, "2017 Vault Rankings: Cravath, Swaine & Moore LLP at a Glance," accessed August 22, 2016, from www.vault.com/company-profiles/law/cravath,-swaine-moore-llp/company-overview.aspx. See also Powell, *BIGLAW*, 65–68; and Joe Patrice, "Biglaw Firm Decimates Summer Associate Program," *Above the Law* (June 30, 2015), accessed November 8, 2015, from http://abovethelaw.com/2015/06/biglaw-firm-decimates-summer-associate-program/.

24. The quote is from a Big Law associate attorney in Powell, *BIGLAW*, 7. See also ibid., 49–64, 68.

25. Wald, "Great Recession and the Legal Profession," 2051, 2055.

26. In 2005, and in line with employment trends of the late twentieth and early twenty-first centuries, law firms were the mainstay for newly licensed attorneys; but at least one empirical study reveals that finding such positions has become more difficult in recent

years, in part as a result of structural changes in the legal marketplace due to the 2008 recession and other factors. Also, from the early to mid-2000s, fewer lawyers were finding work in Big Law firms, and there was a larger concentration of attorneys employed by small firms. Furthermore, the data from 2011 to 2014 indicate that the percentage of solo practitioners grew from 3 to 9 percent. See Deborah Jones Merritt, "What Happened to the Class of 2010? Empirical Evidence of Structural Change in the Legal Profession," *Michigan State Law Review* 2015 (2015): 1043–1123.

27. American Bar Association, "Lawyer Demographics, Year 2016," accessed September 2, 2016, from www.americanbar.org/content/dam/aba/administrative/market_research/lawyer-demographics-tables-2016.authcheckdam.pdf; National Association for Law Placement, "Class of 2015 National Summary Report," accessed September 2, 2016, from www.nalp.org/uploads/NatlSummaryClassof2015.pdf; and National Association for Law Placement, "Prelaw—What Do Lawyers Do?"

28. Herbert M. Kritzer, "The Professions Are Dead, Long Live the Professions: Legal Practice in a Postprofessional World," *Law and Society Review* 33 (1998): 735. See also National Association for Law Placement, "Prelaw—What Do Lawyers Do?"; and National Association for Law Placement, "Class of 2015 National Summary Report."

29. National Association for Law Placement, "Class of 2015 National Summary Report."

30. The promise of indie lawyering is analyzed in Lucille A. Jewel, "Indie Lawyering," in *The Relevant Lawyer: Reimagining the Future of the Legal Profession*, ed. Paul A. Haskins (Chicago, Ill.: ABA Standing Committee on Professionalism, Center for Professional Responsibility, 2015), 113–128; and Lucille A. Jewel, "The Indie Lawyer of the Future: How New Technology, Cultural Trends, and Market Forces Can Transform the Solo Practice of Law," *SMU Science and Technology Law Review* 17 (2014): 325–384. The implications of "disruptive innovation" legal practices, as derived from Harvard Business School professor Clayton Christensen, are discussed in Richard Susskind, *Tomorrow's Lawyers: An Introduction to Your Future* (New York, N.Y.: Oxford University Press, 2013), 39–45; Raymond T. Brescia, "What We Know and Need to Know about Disruptive Innovation," *South Carolina Law Review* 67 (2016): 203–222; and Brian Sheppard, "Incomplete Innovation and the Premature Disruption of Legal Services," *Michigan State Law Review* 2015 (2016): 1797–1910.

31. Joan C. Williams, Aaron Platt, and Jessica Lee, "Disruptive Innovation: New Models of Legal Practice," *Hastings Law Journal* 67 (2016): 1–84.

32. American Bar Association, "Lawyer Demographics, Year 2016"; National Association for Law Placement, "Class of 2015 National Summary Report"; and Merritt, "What Happened to the Class of 2010?," 1078–1080.

33. National Association for Law Placement, "Prelaw—What Do Lawyers Do?" See, generally, Susan Hackett, "Inside Out: An Examination of Demographic Trends in the In-House Profession," *Arizona Law Review* (Fall/Winter 2002): 613.

34. Staci Zaretsky, "Who Are America's Best-Paid General Counsel? (2016)," *Above the Law* (July 18, 2016), accessed September 4, 2016, from http://abovethelaw.com/2016/07/who-are-americas-best-paid-general-counsel-2016/; David Lat, "Who Are America's Best-Paid General Counsel? (2012 Rankings)," *Above the Law* (July 18, 2012), accessed September 4, 2016, from http://abovethelaw.com/2012/07/who-are-americas-best-paid-general-counsel-2012-rankings/. See also Jonathan C. Lipson, Beth Engel, and Jami Crespo, "Who's in the House?: The Changing Nature and Role of In-House and General Counsel," *Wisconsin Law Review* 2012 (2012): 237, 238; Association of Corporate Counsel, "Association of Corporate Counsel Census Reveals Power Shift from Law Firms to Corporate Legal Departments," accessed May 14, 2014, from www.acc.com/aboutacc/newsroom/pressreleases/acc_census_press.cfm; and National Association for Law Placement, "Prelaw—What Do Lawyers Do?"

35. Eli Wald, "In-House Myths," *Wisconsin Law Review* 2012 (2012): 408–462.

36. U.S. Office of Personnel Management, "The Twenty Largest White-Collar Occupations as of September 2012 and Compared to September 2011" and "Number of General Attorneys in Cabinet Level Agencies, Non-seasonal Full-Time Permanent, as of February 2014" (prepared by agency's Data Analysis Group, on file with author). For some of the roles government attorneys play and their unique ethical responsibilities, see Neil M. Peretz, "The Limits of Outsourcing: Ethical Responsibilities of Federal Government Attorneys Advising Executive Branch Officials," *Connecticut Public Interest Law Journal* 6 (2006): 23–63; Anonymous, "Rethinking the Professional Responsibilities of Federal Agency Lawyers," *Harvard Law Review* 115 (2002): 1170–1192; and John C. Yoo, "Lawyers in Congress," *Law and Contemporary Problems* (Spring 1988): 1–19. The professional satisfaction associated with performing public service is discussed in Stephen Breyer, "The Legal Profession and Public Service," *Gauer Distinguished Lecture in Law and Public Policy*, sponsored by the National Legal Center for the Public Interest (New York, N.Y.: September 12, 2000), 9. See also Hope Viner Samborn, "Government Agents: Some Find Perks of Public Sector Work Beat the Potential of Private Practice," *American Bar Association Journal* (December 2002): 64; and Joe D. Whitley, "In the Service of Justice: A U.S. Attorney Defines His Role," *ABA Journal* 79 (1993): 120.

37. William D. Henderson and Leonard Bierman, "An Empirical Analysis of Lateral Lawyer Trends from 2000 to 2007: The Emerging Equilibrium for Corporate Law Firms," *Georgetown Journal of Legal Ethics* 22 (2009): 1395, 1400–1401.

38. Merritt, "What Happened to the Class of 2010?," 1078. See also American Bar Association, "2015 Law Graduate Employment Data," accessed September 4, 2016, from www.americanbar.org/content/dam/aba/administrative/legal_education_and_admis sions_to_the_bar/reports/2015_law_graduate_employment_data.authcheckdam.pdf; National Association for Law Placement, "Class of 2015 National Summary Report"; and National Association for Law Placement, "Prelaw—What Do Lawyers Do?"

39. West, *Teaching Law*, xx. See also National Association for Law Placement, "Class of 2015 National Summary Report."

40. National Association for Law Placement, "Class of 2015 National Summary Report." See also Austin Sarat and Stuart A. Scheingold, eds., *Cause Lawyers and Social Movements.* (Stanford, Calif.: Stanford Law and Politics, 2006); and Catherine R. Albiston and Laura Beth Nielsen, "Funding the Cause: How Public Interest Law Organizations Fund Their Activities and Why It Matters for Social Change," *Law and Social Inquiry* 39 (2014): 62–95.

41. Gita Z. Wilder, *Law School Debt among New Lawyers* (Washington, D.C.: National Association for Legal Career Professionals, 2007), 19; Equal Justice Works, National Association for Law Placement, and Partnership for Public Service, *From the Paper Chase to Money Chase: Law School Debt Diverts Road to Public Service* (Washington, D.C.: Equal Justice Works, NALP, Partnership for Public Service, 2002), 6; see also ABA Commission on Loan Repayment and Forgiveness, *Lifting the Burden: Law Student Debt as a Barrier to Public Service* 10 (Chicago, Ill.: American Bar Association, 2003), 10. Empirical research does not always find that debt is discouraging students from taking public interest jobs. Christa McGill, "Educational Debt and Law Student Failure to Enter Public Service Careers: Bringing Empirical Data to Bear," *Law and Social Inquiry* 31 (2006): 677, 679. An Illinois study, and its findings on the impact of debt on public interest work, is found at Illinois State Bar Association, "Final Report, Findings, and Recommendations on the Impact of Law School Debt on the Delivery of Legal Services" (Adopted by the Assembly of the Illinois State Bar Association, June 22, 2013), accessed May 21, 2014, from www.isba.org/sites/default/files/committees/Law%20School%20 Debt%20Report%20-%203-8-13.pdf, 15–16.

42. See, e.g., Equal Justice Works, "Loan Repayment Assistance Programs," accessed May 21, 2014, from http://equaljusticeworks.org/ed-debt/students/loan-repayment-assistance-programs; Doug Rendleman and Scott Weingart, "Collection of Student Loans," *Washington and Lee Journal of Civil Rights and Social Justice* 20 (2014): 215, 231–234; and Tresa Baldas, "Paying the Way: Loan Programs Booming for Grads in Public Service Jobs," *National Law Journal* (July 5, 2004): 1.

43. Tracey E. George and Albert H. Yoon, "The Labor Market for New Law Professors," *Journal of Empirical Legal Studies* 11 (2014): 1–38. An increasing trend is for law schools to hire JD-PhDs. Lynn M. LoPucki, "Dawn of the Discipline-based Law Faculty," *Journal of Legal Education* 65 (2016): 506–542.

44. Society of American Law Teachers, "2015–16 SALT Salary Survey," *SALT Equalizer 2016* (July 2016), accessed January 1, 2017, from www.saltlaw.org/wp-content/uploads/2015/03/SALT-salary-survey-2016.pdf. Demographic statistics about the composition and total number of law faculty is found in Association of American Law Schools, *Statistical Report on Law School Faculty 2008–09*, accessed February 19, 2017, from https://archives.library.illinois.edu/archon/?p=collections/controlcard&id=10835. See also National Association for Law Placement, "Prelaw—What Do Lawyers Do?"

45. Three elements of law practice—the profession's loss of exclusivity, an increasing segmentation in the application of law knowledge to growing specializations, and the growth of technology to access information resources—combine to create postprofessionalism. Kritzer, *Lawyers at Work*, 319.

46. A "legal information engineer" designs and manages rote legal service delivery systems while providing access to legal information. A "legal consultant" uses specialized knowledge to create protocols for the delivery of legal services that are administered by either legal information engineers or legal processors. A "legal processor" develops or applies specialized services in rote fashion across a wide variety of legal practice areas, such as writing wills, estate planning, or routine civil or criminal matters. Kritzer, *Lawyers at Work*, 321, 323. See also Susskind, *Tomorrow's Lawyers*.

47. Menachem Wecker, "In Tough Job Market, Law Grads Use J.D.s for Nonlegal Work," *U.S. News & World Report* (September 30, 2011), accessed November 9, 2015, from www.usnews.com/education/best-graduate-schools/top-law-schools/articles/2011/09/30/in-tough-job-market-law-grads-use-jds-for-nonlegal-work. See also Debra Cassens Weiss, "'After the JD' Study Shows Many Leave Law Practice," *ABA Journal* 100 (2014): 1; and Hollee Schwartz Temple, "Law Students Prepare for Jobs outside Firms," *ABA Journal* 99 (December 2013): 1.

48. Temple, "Law Students Prepare for Jobs outside Firms."

49. National Association for Law Placement, "Detailed Analysis of JD Advantage Jobs," accessed September 12, 2016, from www.nalp.org/jd_advantage_jobs_detail_may2013.

50. American Bar Association, "2017 Employment Questionnaire (for 2016 Graduates): Definitions and Instructions," accessed February 23, 2017, from www.americanbar.org/content/dam/aba/administrative/legal_education_and_admissions_to_the_bar/Questionnaires/2017_eq_definitions_and_instructions.authcheckdam.pdf.

51. National Association for Law Placement, "Detailed Analysis of JD Advantage Jobs."

52. National Association for Law Placement, "Class of 2015 National Summary Report."

53. Debra Cassens Weiss, "What Kind of Jobs Are JD Advantage?," *American Bar Association Journal* (August 6, 2014), accessed September 12, 2016, from www.abajournal.com/news/article/what_kind_of_jobs_are_jd_advantage/; National Association for Law Placement, "Detailed Analysis of JD Advantage Jobs."

54. See Casey Berman, "Nine Non-legal Jobs You Can (Really, Truly) Do with a Law Degree," *Above the Law* (November 17, 2013), accessed September 12, 2016, from http://abovethelaw.com/career-files/nine-non-legal-jobs-you-can-really-truly-do-with-a-

law-degree/; and Hillary Mantis, "Hot Alternative Legal Careers for 2014," *The National Jurist* (April 15, 2014), accessed September 12, 2016, from www.nationaljurist.com/content/hot-alternative-legal-careers-2014. One legal reformer argues law schools must change their curricula to let graduates gain practice-ready skills in business-related employment, such as in human resources, management analysis, health services, and financial advising. Eric C. Chaffee, "Answering the Call to Reinvent Legal Education: The Need to Incorporate Practical Business and Transactional Skills Training into the Curricula of America's Law Schools," *Stanford Journal of Law, Business and Finance* 20 (2014): 121–178.

55. West, *Teaching Law*, 1 (n. 1). See also ibid., 1–2.

5 Future Trends and Reform Issues in the Legal Profession

There is little doubt that the American legal profession is in a transformative stage of its development. A bevy of scholars argue that the profession is in crisis and in great need of reform for a variety of reasons.[1] It faces many significant challenges for the future. As alluded to in earlier chapters, the legal profession is beset with problems of high tuition rates, student loan debt, declining enrollments, claims of inadequate "practice ready" instruction, Big Law elitism, market instabilities, uncertain employment outlooks, and the widely held perception that law is more of a business than a profession. If the reformers are correct, the legal profession is not only harming itself but also undermining public trust in the legal system.

The criticisms raise systemic questions about whether the legal profession is committed to advancing the rule of law and the goals of justice through the delivery of legal services that are accessible, honest, trustworthy, and for the public good. For some practitioners, these goals and values must not be lost or sacrificed because of the realities of competition and profit-driven behavior that reap only the short-term and shallow comforts of instant gratification.[2] From this perspective, as the profession becomes less "learned," society itself suffers because there is less diversity and commitment to public service, resulting in more indigent *pro se* litigants who are denied equal access to justice because they cannot afford legal aid in criminal prosecutions and civil cases involving basic human needs (e.g., foreclosures, domestic violence, and child custody cases).[3]

This chapter examines these concerns by bringing together the data, trends, and perspectives of the earlier chapters to analyze the challenges of reforming the legal profession. It focuses on the systemic issues that allegedly compromise the ideals underlying it, including facilitating access to justice, performing public service, and achieving a reasonable work–life balance and ultimately professional satisfaction. Three areas of concern are highlighted. They relate to the lack of independent regulatory oversight in governing the legal profession; whether the conventional method of teaching law school doctrine through the casebook method remains viable in light of the high cost of attending law school, the wide availability of uncapped student loans, and uncertain employment prospects in a constrained legal marketplace; and whether technological changes and global competitive pressures are forcing changes in the way law is traditionally practiced in the twenty-first century. These issues are addressed in the next three sections.

THE LEGAL PROFESSION'S INSULARITY

A diffuse collection of federal, state, and local entities govern the regulation of legal education and law practice. These include federal agencies, state licensing authorities, national and state or local bar associations, state judiciaries, and miscellaneous law organizations, groups, or individuals that have vested interests in legal training or law practice. In part prompted by the 2008 recession and the sharp contraction of the legal marketplace in recent years, there are growing criticisms of the regulatory structure of law schools and legal practice.[4]

Understanding and possibly amending the regulatory processes surrounding the profession is important because it controls how lawyers are taught their craft and then assimilated into society for the public good. A common lament is that legal education does not adequately prepare lawyers to practice law or to comprehend what it means to be a professional. Relatedly, the conditions of legal practice are attacked because there is little (or the wrong kind of) regulatory oversight of the types of activities that connect lawyers to the public, such as bar admissions, attorney discipline and malpractice, fees, and advertising, among others.[5]

Underlying the complaints lurks the challenge of moving the legal profession beyond its own occupational interests, a problem reformers assert is due to the profession's rather unique capacity to govern itself with minimal external oversight. In relation to other professions, lawyers have a large degree of unchecked autonomy over their own regulatory practices. Lawyers defend their independence on the grounds that it is necessary to protect clients and the public from the sort of outside interference that will only diminish the profession's core values and practices that are designed to help society. This "traditional" model of the legal profession is based on the notion of a social contract: that is, "in exchange for special expertise, heightened ethical standards, and a devotion to the public interest, lawyers enjoy self-regulatory authority and a state-granted monopoly over legal practice."[6]

Under this model, lawyers restrict entry into the profession and govern themselves independently so that the public is not exposed to unqualified, incompetent, or unethical practitioners.[7] The professional cartel became entrenched early on after lawyers persuaded state licensing officials to adopt the American Bar Association's (ABA) standards for limiting entry into law practice by requiring a legal education, passing a state-administered bar examination, and fulfilling ethical qualifications relating to character and fitness. Other self-regulatory mechanisms, such as passing laws that ban the unauthorized practice of law, and the codification of a single ethical code of conduct (now promulgated as the Model Rules of Professional Conduct), further helped establish the legal profession's insularity, a regulatory tradition that is largely managed by state judiciaries under the inherent powers doctrine.[8]

The denunciation that the legal profession is too insular is accompanied by another criticism that condemns its resistance to look past itself and change for the better. Legal scholar Deborah L. Rhode characterizes this as a "tunnel vision" that shields the profession from unwanted disparagement. If she is correct, public input and governmental action are restricted, which, in turn, reduces lawyer accountability. Without external checks, attorneys "too often lose perspective about the points at which occupational and societal interests conflict."[9] Institutional barriers, including those created by the ABA, are formidable and make the legal profession highly resistant to change.[10] Another impediment, say reformers, is the lack of leadership from law schools that are allegedly detached from the legal profession. The detachment is problematic because law schools are at the forefront of teaching lawyers about their skills and obligations as they are socialized into the profession. Thus, critics assert schools must play a leading role in enacting the type of regulatory reform that fixes what is ailing the legal system.[11] The issue of structurally reforming law school education is discussed next.

Regulating and Reforming Legal Education

With few exceptions, a condition to practicing law is graduating with a three-year juris doctor (JD) degree from an ABA-accredited law school. Under this framework, ABA accreditation standards structurally influence the nature of legal training and the profession as a whole. As professional institutions of higher learning, law schools receive ABA-accreditation approval through a process that is spearheaded by the U.S. Department of Education, a major source of student financial aid. In discharging its functions, the department authorizes six regional higher education accreditation organizations and the ABA Council of the Section of Legal Education and Admissions to the Bar (Council) to establish accreditation standards. Historically, the national and state governments involved in higher education accreditation have taken a hands-off, or deferential, approach in supervising the educational institutions they are monitoring, opting instead to give universities and colleges significant discretion to fashion performance and quality enhancement indicators through self-studies and peer review evaluations.[12]

Law school accreditation evolved differently, so its regulatory processes are distinctive. The first step in the evolutionary process was the Council's declaration of its first accreditation standards in the early 1920s. Over the next seventy years, the Council's accrediting role expanded. During that time, it consisted of a majority of legal educators (deans and faculty) who sat alongside other lawyers and judges who represented a minority. But, due to changes in federal law and a 1995 antitrust lawsuit filed by the Department of Justice against the ABA, the Council (and its Accreditation and Standards Review Committees) was legally forced to restrict the number of legal educators who served on the Council or its committees; and the ABA's main governance unit, its House of Delegates, could no longer be the final authority in making decisions about accreditation. With fewer legal academics on the Council, law school accreditation is differentiated from higher education accreditation that traditionally uses peer reviews from educators as the baseline for earning accreditation. In addition, the Council has interpreted its standards to mean that judgments about whether law schools are enhancing the quality of their programs are left to the law schools themselves. Thus, while regional authorities provide some oversight of the law school accreditation process, as a practical matter the Council is the sole accrediting entity that sets the standards that schools must comply with in order to receive ABA approval and federal financial aid. Moreover, law schools wield significant power in shaping the quality of their programs to meet the Council's accreditation standards.[13]

For critics, this double insularity, which gives the Council and law schools extraordinary influence in shaping and meeting accreditation standards, is untenable.[14]

A Council composed mostly of lawyers and judges with no academic experience cannot render independent peer assessments about the quality of law school programs that should be protecting the public interest. As Rhode puts it, "However well intentioned, no occupational group is well positioned to make disinterested judgments on matters where its own livelihood is so directly implicated."[15] In addition, giving law schools virtually unbridled discretion to mold their own legal programs does not incentivize them to structure their curriculum in a way that enhances new lawyer competencies in a rapidly evolving and highly competitive twenty-first-century legal marketplace.

As a result, law school accreditation standards, which measure educational "inputs" (such as classroom hours, three years of postgraduate study, student–faculty ratios, library and physical plant resources, restrictions on teaching online courses and using adjunct faculty, and the size and research productivity of high-salary tenured faculty), have acquired a costly "one-size-fits-all accreditation framework" that hampers curricular innovation, experimentation, and diversity.[16] The lack of creativity also comes at a high price to students who have limited capacity to make informed decisions about quality of law schools or their cost-effectiveness. Furthermore, students are not being taught the essential skills of professionalism or legal practice, and worse, they are forced to subsidize expensive legal academic programs and law school faculty with high tuition bills and unmanageable student loan debt.[17]

Although a 2009 U.S. Government Accountability Office report concluded that an undue reliance on the *U.S. News & World Report* rankings, and not simply law school accreditation standards, triggered rising law school tuition rates, the 2014 ABA Task Force on the Future of Legal Education (Task Force) recommended to the Council that it alter its standards to reduce their uniformity in an effort to grow curricular heterogeneity, improve lawyer competencies, and cut costs. As the Task Force observed, "The accreditation system . . . imposes requirements that increase costs without conferring commensurate benefits [and it] would better serve the public interest by enabling more heterogeneity in law schools and by encouraging more attention to services, outcomes, and value delivered to law students."[18]

In response, the Council overhauled its 2014 standards to adopt select "outcome" measures of learning and teaching performance, such as requiring an experiential six credits of learning courses (via a simulation course, a law clinic, or a field placement) and empirical data of bar passage rates. Under the revisions, law schools are obliged to create learning outcomes standards that are tied to the school's academic purpose and mission, a move designed to enhance ethics and professionalism training. New assessment and feedback criteria were introduced, so schools must demonstrate what their students have learned. The outcome and assessment approach means that law schools must provide evidence of compliance when they write their self-study reports that are part of the accreditation evaluations. Moreover, the new standards mandate that quality of instruction must improve, so simply showing that they are retaining minimal educational standards will not be enough.[19]

Since then, however, some law schools have come under fire for misrepresenting their employment or lawyer salary statistics and admitting unqualified applicants in an effort to boost their declining enrollments. The sharp reduction in enrollments has been accompanied by a nationwide drop in bar passage rates and additional allegations that law schools are exploiting students who can borrow up to the full cost of their tuition and living expenses due to a 2006 change in federal student loan law that allows them to do so. Consequently, some law schools are embroiled in ongoing litigation, and the Council is moving toward making further revisions to its accreditation standards.[20] The changes that are likely to be implemented according to the 2016 standards include (1) requiring law schools to show that 75 percent of their students passed the bar exam within two years and (2) creating a presumption that law schools with an attrition rate above 20 percent are not in compliance with a standard requiring them to only admit students who appear capable of successfully graduating and passing the bar examination.[21]

For some advocacy groups, such as Law School Transparency (LST), these revisions do not go far enough. Among other things, LST urges that the Council adopt an 85 percent bar passage rate and require empirical evidence from over seventy at-risk law schools that shows their students can graduate and pass the bar. Also, it argues that law schools that remain noncompliant must lose their accreditation or face public sanctions.[22] For still other reformers, the Council must amend its bylaws to permit a larger proportion of legal educators to sit on the Council as well as on its Accreditation Committee, especially since it already does not restrict how many can serve on its Standards Committee. Doing so will infuse peer governance and higher academic quality into the law school accreditation process. As a former Council member explains, "It is time for legal education to embrace a system of accreditation that is grounded on peer assessment, dedicated to improving—and not just assessing—the quality of legal education, and guided by the same peer governance structure that has worked so well in the rest of American higher education."[23]

Reforming legal education is only realistic if law schools are receptive to change. Yet, as with the organized bar, the insularity of the legal education establishment suggests that law schools will not alter their curricula unless they are compelled to do so by the federal government and outside accrediting bodies or state licensing entities. The steps taken by the Council in tightening accreditation requirements suggest that law schools will have to adjust their existing programs to earn accreditation. Additionally, some states have begun to alter their licensing requirements, which, in turn, will influence law school curriculum reform. State officials are now compelling students to take preadmission courses in professional responsibility, or to show that their training includes specific knowledge about instructional methodologies, the law of the state, or new lawyer competencies. In New Hampshire, licensing authorities created a Daniel Webster Scholar alternative licensing program that permits graduates to practice law once they receive training on substantive law and practice-ready skills, including listening, problem solving, ethics, negotiation, advisement, and professionalism. Other innovations include offering course credit for performing fifty hours of *pro bono* work that must be completed before sitting for the bar examination in New York; and, in California, bar licensing is conditional upon the completion of a preadmission competency training program.[24]

Regulating and Reforming Legal Practice Conditions

The problem of insularity in the American legal profession is relevant to the regulatory structures surrounding the delivery of legal services once bar passage is achieved. Today, the conditions of legal practice that connect the public to lawyers are managed by the ethical rules created by the ABA and implemented and enforced by state judiciaries and state or local bar organizations. The Model Rules of Professional Conduct, which have been adopted by state courts with little revision, dictate where lawyers can practice, how they can deliver legal services, and in what manner they can be held accountable through disciplinary actions and rules. Lawyers defend the rules because rules safeguard the public from incompetent lawyers who are unqualified to practice law. Still, the rules tend to isolate the legal profession from outside forces and protect lawyers from economic competition that threatens to usurp their established role in society and diminish the profits they reap. In this light, the organized bar has been reluctant to revise the regulatory structures governing legal practice. Still, the rapid transformation of technologies, the realities of the legal marketplace, and the strong demand to provide better access to justice for those who need it are increasing pressures that may prompt future regulatory reform.[25]

For critics, the bar's regulatory structure is out of sync with today's rapidly evolving legal marketplace, a problem that reduces access to justice and degrades the legal profession's commitment to public service and professionalism. A frequent reform target is altering the "geo-centric" traditional model of lawyer regulation that geographically situates legal practice within a specific state, the location where lawyers are credentialed to practice. A related prohibition bars nonlawyers from delivering legal services. Thus, in light of market realities, shifting client preferences and demands, and the growth of Internet-based platforms, reform is directed at easing restrictions on certain nonlawyer aspects of legal practice. Reform advocates also insist that the bar change its regulations to increase access to justice by strengthening the requirements for continuing education, performing public service, and remaining ethical under the threat of disciplinary sanctions.[26]

Multijurisdictional and Multidisciplinary Practice

Reformers argue that preventing lawyers from practicing law in multiple states, or in employment situations that involve fee sharing with nonlawyers (such as accountants), is an outdated approach to contemporary legal practice. Changes in technology warrant that lawyers ought to be permitted to deliver "U.S. cross-border" and global legal services with less restriction. Today, attorneys perform legal services by phone, email, fax, or online in the United States and globally. Thus, unless there is a need to have physical presence, such as representing a client in court, there is little justification for barring representation that can be accomplished by virtual realities and means. In the exceptional circumstances that require physical presence, existing *pro hac vice* rules can be used to let out-of-state counsel enlist the help of a local attorney to perform the required legal services. So, reformers argue that the ethical rules that bar the unauthorized practice of law ought to be changed to permit out-of-state lawyers to practice law across jurisdictional borders either by passing a national bar examination or by using an open-border admission process that permits one state to test lawyer competence but requires other states to respect that judgment under certain conditions. A similar argument calls for easing the restrictions on multidisciplinary practice; that is, due to a growing demand in the global legal marketplace, the U.S. bar must align itself with other western industrialized nations that allow nonlawyers, such as large global accounting firms and other key businesses that interact with the legal industry, to perform work with attorneys.[27]

Nonlawyer Investment

Traditionally, law firms operate through partnership or related agreements that fund the business through profits or loans by the firm's partners or outside banks. Whether law firms remain financially stable or can expand their operations depends on, and is limited to, the capital investments partners can make to the business enterprise. While this model arguably works best in small law firms, larger firms that seek to practice law domestically or across the globe face monetary constraints that prevent them from expanding their businesses or attracting the interest of outside investors because ethical rules prohibit nonlawyers from making financial investments in law firms. Limiting investments to lawyers "in house" is also defended on the grounds that exposing a firm's balance sheet, client lists, and work details to nonlawyer outside funders protects lawyer independence, prevents conflicts of interest, and preserves client confidentiality.[28]

On the other hand, reformers insist that the ban on nonlawyer investment inhibits an infusion of private capital or equity that could be used to enlarge a law firm's capacity to amass the types of resources it needs to remain competitive in an evolving U.S. and global legal economy. While reformers concede that some regulation of nonlawyer investment is necessary (such as limiting investment to a certain percentage and/or requiring investors to meet character fitness tests), they observe that the ABA Commission on Ethics 20/20 studied the issue and did not find any evidence of disciplinary problems that emerged in the District of Columbia, a jurisdiction that has permitted nonlawyer investments in law firms for the past twenty years. Also, they argue that such "alternative business structures" (ABS) have been in successful operation in Australia and England (and Wales), provided they are subject to the same type of ethical restrictions that are imposed on lawyers. Under this view, not only do ABS facilitate a firm's business productivity, but they also offer benefits to consumers by giving them "additional choice, greater price and quality competition, more non-lawyer expertise and resources, and increased access and convenience from one-stop shopping and economies of scale."[29]

Professional Competence and Lawyer Discipline

Another set of regulatory structures that critics question relates to lawyer competence and discipline. While state courts are entrusted to enforce the code of ethics, they show great deference to the organized bar as a general matter. Although a majority of states require that attorneys complete roughly a dozen hours of continuing legal education (CLE) every year, CLE obligations remain negligible, easy, and substantively meaningless in practice. Earning CLE is often a function of lawyer representations of self-study because the bar associations that host CLE courses usually do not have the resources to put quality control measures in place to ensure compliance, such as self-monitoring verification procedures, checking attendance at seminars, or administering an exam. The subject matter of CLE is lacking as well since training is not given on the issues that cause most disciplinary problems, like neglecting a client, engaging in financial mismanagement, charging excessive fees, or not preparing a case well; and there is little demonstrable research that indicates CLE actually improves attorney competencies in practice.[30]

Without more rigorous oversight and substantive content, reformers assert that the minimal requirements of CLE are reduced to a token public relations exercise that only benefits the bar associations that collect the fees and the convention centers that host the CLE courses. In this light, legal scholar Rhode quotes a veteran attorney as saying, "Almost any lawyer will tell you [that] CLE credits are much easier to swallow when washed down with Bloody Mary's." For Rhode, a pilot program in New York City is a model for reform: its New Lawyer Institute features "mentoring as well as a year-long curriculum including programs targeted to practical skills, nuts-and-bolts practice management, and career development." Or, states could make CLE mandatory for new attorneys or for those who have been sanctioned for disciplinary or malpractice reasons. Alternatively, in voluntary CLE jurisdictions, lawyers can receive CLE certifications by taking an exam showing their competencies, which then can be incorporated into their professional portfolios and marketing practices.[31]

Apart from CLE issues, the autonomy of lawyers in disciplining themselves for ethical misconduct also has been reviewed critically. Each state has the discretion to license, regulate, and discipline lawyer conduct. Under the inherent powers doctrine, state supreme courts are tasked with the administrative duty to use ethical codes to determine rule violations and to deliver appropriate sanctions. Yet the procedural machinery behind filing, investigating, and resolving client grievances is decentralized, secret, cumbersome, and not user-friendly. The federal government does not operate a uniform database of attorney misconduct. Although the ABA maintains a National Lawyer Regulatory Data Bank as a national registry of public disciplinary sanctions against U.S. lawyers, only savvy clients are aware of the repository's existence or actually take advantage of it—but only after paying a fee that yields a report about the sanctions levied against individual attorneys (not law firms) that is submitted to the Data Bank on a *voluntary* basis by state courts. In addition, clients who are harmed by attorneys who are licensed in multiple states face even more hurdles to discover the full scope of a lawyer's misfeasance.[32]

At the state level, very few states require that lawyers maintain malpractice insurance; and, in states with voluntary compliance, the rate of coverage can be surprisingly low. For example, Illinois merely requires that its attorneys *disclose* if they have malpractice coverage; and, in 2015, only 52 percent of 94,128 registered lawyers reported that they actually had it.[33] Furthermore, clients often must air their grievances through an elaborate bureaucratic process that is managed for the most part by lawyers and judges. In Ohio, the disciplinary process involves many procedural steps: (1) complaints are submitted to a state disciplinary council or grievance committee; (2) if those bodies validate that there is substantial credible evidence of misconduct, a formal complaint is forwarded to a Board of Professional Conduct panel to determine probable cause; (3) if probable cause is found, the complaint is sent to the Board of Professional Conduct; (4) if the lawyer files an answer to the allegations, a three-member panel from the board holds a hearing and makes a recommendation to the full board about how to dispose of the complaint; and (5) the Supreme Court issues a final decision after getting the board's recommendation. While each state varies in operating its own disciplinary system, the basic steps of inquiry, investigation, formal filing, hearing and review, and final disposition by the state's highest court are a common template. Arguably, the bureaucratic complexities of the disciplinary process seem more intent on protecting attorneys' due process and reputation as opposed to resolving client interests and disputes.[34]

The minimal effectiveness of self-monitoring disciplinary systems is registered by the fact that only the most egregious ethical violations are actually sanctioned by state courts. A review of annual disciplinary reports from states with some of the highest numbers of practicing lawyers indicates that the vast majority of complaints by clients are dismissed in the initial stages of disciplinary review; and, of the cases that move forward, a small percentage of attorneys are formally sanctioned (i.e., by public reprimand, suspension, or disbarment).[35] Also, as critics have alleged, the reports suggest that state disciplinary processes are burdened with problems of limited resources, high caseloads, delay, backlog, transparency, and accountability. To illustrate, in response to a state auditor's report, *State Bar of California: It Has Not Consistently Protected the Public through Its Attorney Discipline Process and Lacks Accountability*, the State Bar of California was compelled to report additional data on the backlog of cases and the speed with which it handled complaints because the auditor found that the state bar "has frequently changed its criteria and methodologies for how it gathers the information included in its discipline reports and, more importantly, did not always fully disclose the changes made in its criteria and methodologies."[36] Also, many states, such as New York, generally treat disciplinary proceedings as private and confidential matters unless a formal action was heard by the court; thus in the majority of instances the public only gets to learn about the most egregious (or criminal) conduct by attorneys that is most likely to result in formal sanctions.[37]

While critics acknowledge that some miscreant lawyers remain subject to discipline, the insularity of the disciplinary process, when combined with the lack of nonlegal government oversight and the bureaucratic complexities of investigating and sanctioning misconduct, makes it difficult for injured clients to get full vindication of their complaints in a timely, efficient, and transparent manner. A number of remedial steps could be taken to improve lawyer accountability and professionalism, including requiring lawyers to carry malpractice insurance and expanding the jurisdiction of disciplinary bodies to review the types of client complaints that occur most frequently, such as attorney neglect and fee disputes. Moreover, state officials can mandate that lawyers report their records of disciplinary action into a centralized database that becomes open for public inspection once probable cause is established after an investigation.[38] The professed need to reform the conditions of legal practice also coincides with similar arguments to change legal instruction that has too become ossified, and inadequate, to train lawyers to practice law in today's society.

THE DIFFICULTIES OF TRADITIONAL LAW SCHOOL INSTRUCTION

The debate over the structure, quality, and practicality of legal instruction is a longstanding controversy in the legal academy.[39] The debate centers on whether the doctrinal casebook method of law training is an incomplete pedagogy that is ill suited to teach students legal practice and professional identity skills. While the introduction of the casebook method in the late nineteenth century was revolutionary for its time, reformers assert that its doctrinal, case dialogue delivery of legal knowledge in an unstructured curriculum is only relevant today for learning analytical skills of reasoning and logic. For critics, simply learning how to "think like a lawyer" is pedagogically indefensible: (1) the teacher-oriented and case-based approach is out of step with higher education norms that use student-centered pedagogies, such as experiential learning with outcomes and assessments, as intellectual baselines for achieving student success; (2) students are taught law by faculty who have limited or no experience practicing law, and who have not received any formal training in educational theory beyond what they picked up in earning their own JD degree; (3) the focus on legal doctrine ignores larger questions of social justice and the role that interdisciplinary subjects (history, political science, economics, and the like) play in shaping and determining the law's meaning and application in society; and (4) testing legal doctrine by using a single, semester-end examination may be not only discriminatory but also psychologically harmful to students. As one legal expert put it, the traditional model of legal instruction is deeply flawed because students "may have learned to 'think like a lawyer' but not how to make a living at it."[40]

Although several studies commissioned by different entities within the legal profession have proposed reforms that incorporate more clinical training and experiential learning methods, the organized bar, law schools, and the judiciary have been reluctant, and sometimes hostile, to embrace or implement them fully.[41] The proposals for reform are wide ranging. They include, among others, revamping the third year of instruction by making it more clinically based, or the focus of an internship; ending the third year of law school and granting a two-year law degree; revising the law school curriculum and pedagogies to include more "practice ready" courses and experiential or online learning; infusing law faculties with teachers who have more practical experience or advanced degrees, including PhDs; and revising (or eliminating) the existing format of the bar examination, which, for some critics, "tests too much and too little."[42]

In addition, the issue of whether law schools ought to revise their pedagogy and curriculum has also been the focus of an assessment by the 2014 ABA Task Force on the Future of Legal Education (Task Force). Along with recommending that law schools revise their programs with new accreditation standards that are more responsive to learning outcomes and assessments, the Task Force criticized law schools for attracting highly qualified students (with the best LSAT scores and UGPAs) with offers of scholarships that do not take into account financial need. This widespread recruitment practice not only leads to higher tuition rates, but also forces the rest of the incoming class to not receive tuition discounts, which makes less qualified students rely extensively on student loans that are easily available under federal law. Legal education's pricing and funding system, therefore, decreases student body and legal profession diversity as well as exacerbates pervasive student debt and high tuition rate problems.[43]

The Task Force concludes that law schools must do more than offer doctrinal legal training to students because it is unsatisfactory to teach students how to practice law or assume professional roles. The findings reiterate those made by former District of Columbia circuit judge Harry T. Edwards who pointed out as early as 1992 that there was a great divide between the teaching and practice of law.

In explaining the gap, Edwards argued that law schools overemphasize the pursuit of academic theory while law firms are unduly preoccupied with the pursuit of profit. As a result, the "middle ground—ethical practice—has been deserted by both." Legal instruction, therefore, must help students to develop the skill of making professional judgments about which clients to serve and how to represent them as an officer of the court in the client's and public interest.[44] Further, while Edwards is supportive of doctrinal training in the first year since it instills the capacity to use the law in their work, he maintains that students must also be taught "the art of legal practice" through clinical courses that should be taken in the second year. For Edwards, a third year of law school might not even be necessary to accomplish these goals; and the case dialogue method that is typically used to convey doctrinal instruction can be modified or replaced with experiential learning exercises that teach students, preferably in smaller classes, how to interpret and apply the law to real-life client situations. Under this view, the premise of legal scholarship (law reviews that are generally not subject to external peer review) that is published by law faculty is seriously called into question. While there is some value to "abstract scholarship," most of it is impractical because the "work is not useful to most practicing lawyers, legislators, judges, and regulators who employ the law to promote societal well-being." Students, therefore, derive no benefit from it since it does not give them any insight about the law's purpose and what lawyers are supposed to do as public servants. In this light, Chief Justice John G. Roberts Jr.'s musings about the utility of legal scholarship in 2011 are telling: "What the academy is doing, as far as I can tell, is largely of no use or interest to people who actually practice law." Perhaps more significantly, the ABA's Task Force underscored that legal education is part of the private marketplace, so "law schools may have to respond to consumer preferences, irrespective of the preferences of those within the law school, at least in order to ensure the continued financial stability of their programs."[45]

The Task Force's warning notably explains why the legal academy has traditionally resisted changing the pedagogical status quo. In defending their academic mission, law faculties argue their research has significant public value. They dismiss the notion that their work ought to center on legal practice because doing so reduces law schools to trade schools. From this perspective, reforming legal education is repugnant: that is, "law practitioners [are] several cuts below plumbers in both the intellectual challenge and moral utility of their work." Other critics, such as Seventh Circuit judge Richard Posner, add that legal scholarship's usefulness does not have to cater to specific audiences, such as practitioners; and, regardless, its public value is evidenced by its interdisciplinary impact on shaping the law's meaning in various areas of jurisprudence, such as election law (political science), legal procedure and evidence (psychology), First Amendment speech (legal feminism), and constitutional and statutory interpretation (philosophy, literary, and political theory).[46]

The disagreement over reform is important because any effort to implement it will necessitate making significant changes to law school culture, institutional norms, and financial realities. Whether legal education is thought of as a public good or a private commodity is not merely an academic debate. As the Task Force recognized, altering the traditional model of instruction by incorporating more clinical and experiential learning threatens tenure-track faculty whose careers are structured by tenure, promotion, and retention guidelines that reward productive doctrine-based legal scholarship. Reform that attaches a private value to legal education will in all likelihood compel tenured or tenure-track faculty to adjust not only their approach to teaching and research, but also their professional lifestyles and reputational status expectations. As one law professor candidly acknowledged, being more attentive to budgetary matters might entail that law faculty "cut the cost of legal scholarship by cutting back on some of the luxuries that surround it," such as attending expensive and fully paid-for academic workshops that are held in multiple law schools to deliver presentations relating to the publication of law review articles.[47] Nevertheless, the Task Force flatly asserted that there must be a "re-orientation of attitudes toward change, including market-driven change, by persons within the school," a daunting task because many law faculty "find their positions especially attractive because they are largely outside market- and change-driven environments."[48]

THE COMPETITIVE DELIVERY OF LEGAL SERVICES IN THE FUTURE

In recent years, new constraints have emerged that affect the economies of law practice in the twenty-first century. Their presence has forced the legal profession to reassess traditional business models and established norms for delivering legal services. Corporate clientele and individual consumers are acutely interested in getting value for the legal products they pay for, a trend that legal scholar Richard Susskind labels the "More-for-Less Challenge."[49] On the supply side, in-house counsel and Big Law firms are more attuned to cutting costs, which has led them to downsize legal departments, hire fewer law graduates, and outsource (or in-house) their legal work to cheaper "alternative legal providers" and vendors (like Rocket Lawyer, Avvo, or LegalZoom) that have assumed a prominent spot in an intensely competitive legal marketplace. In some instances, fee structures are being adjusted to move away from a billable hour system in favor of incorporating fixed-cost, or capped (which puts a limit on how much is paid), fee arrangements. At the ground level, students matriculating into law school and new law graduates increasingly worry that they will not be able to launch a legal career in private practice or sometimes not even find a job at the end of an expensive law school journey, a prospect that sharpens the demands for more "practice ready" or "practice aware," or alternative career, professional training.[50]

For Susskind and other reformers, the "More-for-Less Challenge," along with the rapid and powerful growth of information technology and a global-inspired trend to ease restrictions on who can provide legal services (other than those "authorized" to practice law, as in the United States), is a significant change agent that will redefine the contours of law practice in the future.[51] Susskind predicts that "[i]n the long run, increasing amounts of legal work can and will be taken on by advanced computer systems, with a light hand on the tiller from the human beings who are their users." Consequently, traditional Big Law firm practices of using a legion of associate attorneys to perform document reviews (for litigation purposes) or do basic contract drafting will eventually yield to "information systems that can outperform junior lawyers and administrative staff." Or, law firms may opt to create teams of partner-lawyers who enlist a single associate attorney assistant to help them on legal projects and, if needed, outsource basic tasks to external vendors. Still another variation envisions law firms creating teams of paralegals or other professionals to manage data and files in a standardized and systematic fashion that reduces costs and increases efficiency.[52]

While there will always be a need for conventional lawyers (and law training), Susskind argues that there will be a growing market for "more flexible, team-based, hybrid-professionals" who can use their legal skills to manage, review, analyze, and solve problems in technologically sophisticated and diverse entrepreneurial settings. Within companies and law firms, such lawyers can assume positions as legal knowledge engineers, legal technologists, legal project managers, legal management consultants, and legal risk managers, among others. Lawyers in those employment roles will be attractive to global accounting firms (e.g., modeled after Anderson Advisors, a large law firm providing tax accounting services), premier legal publishers (e.g., Thomson Reuters and RELX Group), legal process outsourcers (e.g., businesses, typically located in India, doing rote legal work such as document reviews or drafting simple contracts), legal leasing agencies (e.g., Axiom, which supplies temporary services on a contract and project basis), online legal service providers (e.g., that churn out online legal documents or undertake online dispute resolution services, such as arbitration or mediation), and traditional businesses that require complex legal management advice or consultation.[53]

The broad impact of Internet technologies and persistent globalization pressures on the legal industry has captured the attention of the ABA Commission on the Future of Legal Services (Commission). After a two-year study, the Commission's August 2016 report determined that a large majority of less wealthy citizens in the United States cannot afford, or lack knowledge about, legal services, a problem that reformers have dubbed "the justice gap," or "civil Gideon" (a movement arguing that low-income clients must be given greater access to the justice system as a right in certain civil cases that implicate basic human needs, such as domestic abuse, child custody, or foreclosure cases).[54] In so finding, the Commission explained that courts, bar associations, law schools, and lawyers are beginning to use creatively different facets of technology to deliver legal services with remote access technologies, online legal resource centers, incubator (business entrepreneurial training) programs, legal process outsourcing, and automated document assembly systems, to name a few.[55]

Yet, some legal observers contend that the Commission did not go far enough in providing clarity or specific guidance to the legal profession about the steps it must take to bridge the justice gap. For instance, the report did not explicitly support non-lawyer ownership of law firms; rather, it recommended that the judiciary endorse an earlier ABA resolution that did not favor it. Also, although the Commission cited the successful impact of legal service providers, it merely recommended that courts and states only continue to consider the issue of whether it is best to promulgate rules and procedures that allow for their wider adoption within the legal profession. As one legal commentator concluded, the report was more helpful in defining the problems of lack of access than in proposing solutions that increase access to justice in light of technological changes. Simply put, while the report noted the key issues of "evolving business models, evolving service-delivery models, and emerging technologies," the Commission failed in "taking bold and decisive stands, instead recommending further study and consideration." In this respect, it is not surprising, but ironic, that the Commission declared that "[t]he legal profession continues to resist change, not only to the public's detriment but also its own."[56]

CONCLUSION

The challenges facing the American legal profession have caused it to look inward in attempting to strike a balance of reform that best accommodates its traditional interests and professional ideals. As this chapter demonstrates, the profession's insularity, when combined with the market demands placed on legal educators and lawyer practitioners who vie to remain competitive in a twenty-first century highlighted by rapid technological changes, is a formidable obstacle to effectuating reform. For reform to succeed, all facets of the American legal profession—the organized bar, state judiciaries, the legal academy, and lawyers themselves—must elevate the public's interest in securing access to justice above the profession's vested or entrenched interests that undermine the commitment to the rule of law and rendering legal services in a reasonable and equitable fashion.

SELECTED READINGS

American Bar Association Commission on the Future of Legal Services. *Report on the Future of Legal Services in the United States.* Chicago, Ill.: American Bar Association, 2016. Available at http://abafuturesreport.com/#1.

American Bar Association Task Force on the Future of Legal Education. *Report and Recommendations.* Chicago, Ill.: American Bar Association, January 2014. Available at www.americanbar.org/content/dam/aba/administrative/professional_responsibility/report_and_recommendations_of_aba_task_force.authcheckdam.pdf.

Haskins, Paul A., ed. *The Relevant Lawyer: Reimagining the Future of the Legal Profession.* Chicago, Ill.: American Bar Association Center for Professional Responsibility, 2015.

Kronman, Anthony. *The Lost Lawyer: Failing Ideals of the Legal Profession.* Cambridge, Mass.: Belknap Press of Harvard University Press, 1993.

Levit, Nancy, and Douglas O. Linder. *The Happy Lawyer: Making a Good Life in the Law.* New York, N.Y.: Oxford University Press, 2010.

Susskind, Richard. *Tomorrow's Lawyers: An Introduction to Your Future.* New York, N.Y.: Oxford University Press, 2013.

WEB LINKS

American Bar Association (www.americanbar.org)

Institute for the Advancement of the American Legal System (http://iaals.du.edu/educating-tomorrows-lawyers/projects/resources/legal-profession)

Law.com (www.law.com)

Law School Transparency (www.lawschooltransparency.com)

ENDNOTES

1. Deborah L. Rhode, *The Trouble with Lawyers* (New York, N.Y.: Oxford University Press, 2015); Benjamin H. Barton, *Glass Half Full: The Decline and Rebirth of the Legal Profession* (New York, N.Y.: Oxford University Press, 2015); William Domnarski, *Swimming in Deep Water: Lawyers, Judges, and Our Troubled Legal Profession* (Chicago, Ill.: American Bar Association, 2014); Robin L. West, *Teaching Law: Justice, Politics, and the Demands of Professionalism* (New York, N.Y.: Cambridge University Press, 2013); Steven J. Harper, *The Lawyer Bubble* (New York, N.Y.: Basic Books, 2013); James E. Moliterno, *The American Legal Profession in Crisis: Resistance and Responses to Change* (New York, N.Y.: Oxford University Press, 2010); Thomas D. Morgan, *The Vanishing Lawyer* (New York, N.Y.: Oxford University Press, 2010); Douglas Litowitz, *The Destruction of Young Lawyers: Beyond One L* (Akron, Ohio: University of Akron Press, 2006); Anthony Kronman, *The Lost Lawyer: Failing Ideals of the Legal Profession* (Cambridge, Mass.: Belknap Press of Harvard University Press, 1993).

2. William C. Hubbard, "Foreword," in *The Relevant Lawyer: Reimagining the Future of the Legal Profession*, ed. Paul A. Haskins (Chicago, Ill.: American Bar Association Center for Professional Responsibility, 2015), xvii.

3. See Rhode, *Trouble with Lawyers*, 146–149.

4. See Sarah Valentine, "Flourish or Founder: The New Regulatory Regime in Legal Education," *Journal of Law and Education* 44 (2015): 473, 476 (n. 12).

5. Deborah L. Rhode, *In the Interests of Justice: Reforming the Legal Profession* (New York, N.Y.: Oxford University Press, 2000), 143. See also Valentine, "Flourish or Founder," 476.

6. Dana A. Remus, "Out of Practice: The Twenty-first-Century Legal Profession," *Duke Law Journal* 63 (2014): 1243, 1248.

7. Ibid., 1247–1249.

8. Ibid., 1249–1251. See also Charles W. Wolfram, "Lawyer Turf and Lawyer Regulation: The Role of the Inherent-Powers Doctrine," *University of Arkansas at Little Rock Law Journal* 12 (1989): 1, 6–16.

9. Rhode, *In the Interests of Justice*, 144.

10. Sheldon Krantz, *The Legal Profession: What Is Wrong and How to Fix It* (New Providence, N.J.: LexisNexis, 2014), 129.

11. Rhode, *In the Interests of Justice,* 186. See also Krantz, *Legal Profession,* 115, 123–125.

12. Judith Areen, "Accreditation Reconsidered," *Iowa Law Review* (2011): 1472, 1473–1474, 1479.

13. Ibid., 1488–1491.

14. Rhode, *Trouble with Lawyers*, 127–129; Rhode, *In the Interests of Justice,* 187–192; Areen, "Accreditation Reconsidered," 1485–1491.

15. Rhode, *Trouble with Lawyers*, 128.

16. Rhode, *In the Interests of Justice,* 189–190; Rhode, *Trouble with Lawyers,* 121–122.

17. Rhode, *In the Interests of Justice,* 190–191. See also James Podgers, "Law School Accreditation Standards Get Update after 6 Years of Effort," *ABA Journal* 100 (October 2014): 1 (reporting that an ABA consultant in the Legal Education Section in 2014 stated that high tuition rates are caused by decreasing state support of public law schools, a reduction in student–faculty ratios, and an increase in the number of tenure-track and adjunct faculty).

18. American Bar Association Task Force on the Future of Legal Education, *Report and Recommendations* (January 2014), accessed June 10, 2016, from www.americanbar.org/content/dam/aba/administrative/professional_responsibility/report_and_recommendations_of_aba_task_force.authcheckdam.pdf. See also Government Accountability Office,

Issues Related to Law School Cost and Access (October 2009), accessed June 10, 2016, from www.gao.gov/products/A88198.

19. Valentine, "Flourish or Founder," 507–514. The 2013–2014, 2014–2015, 2015–2016, and 2016–2017 standards and summaries and how to interpret them are found in American Bar Association Section of Legal Education and Admissions to the Bar, "ABA Standards," accessed March 1, 2017, from www.americanbar.org/groups/legal_education/resources/standards.html.

20. In 2006, Congress extended the federal Direct PLUS Loan program to allow a graduate or professional student to borrow the full amount of tuition and living expenses. In 2014, the Obama administration enacted regulations (called the gainful employment rule) that deny federal student aid money to for-profit schools that cannot show that they success-fully prepared graduates for jobs that will let them pay back their loans. Editorial Board, "The Law School Debt Crisis," *New York Times* (October 24, 2014), accessed February 23, 2017, from www.nytimes.com/2015/10/25/opinion/sunday/the-law-school-debt-crisis.html. In 2014, there were 3,700 fewer law school applicants than in 2013, and schools experienced a drop of at least 8,000 in the three previous years. Natalie Kitroeff, "Law School Applications to Set 15-Year Low," *Bloomberg* (March 15, 2015), accessed June 10, 2016, from www.bloomberg.com/news/articles/2015-03-19/law-school-applications-will-hit-their-lowest-point-in-15-years. In 2014 and 2015, there was a nationwide drop in bar passage rates. Mark Hansen, "Proposals to Amend Law School Accreditation Standards Would Require More Focus on Grads' Bar Passage," *ABA Journal* (June 2016): 22.

21. Hansen, "Proposals to Amend Law School Accreditation Standards," 22. See also Sudhin Thanawala, "Lawsuits Part of Call for More Transparency at Law Schools," *U.S. News & World Report* (December 6, 2015), accessed June 10, 2016, from www.usnews.com/news/us/articles/2015/12/06/lawsuits-part-of-call-for-more-transparency-at-law-schools.

22. Law School Transparency, "2015 State of Legal Education, Key Findings," accessed June 10, 2016, from www.lawschooltransparency.com/reform/projects/investigations/2015/key-findings/.

23. Areen, "Accreditation Reconsidered," 1494.

24. Valentine, "Flourish or Founder," 480–481, 515–524.

25. Rhode, *Trouble with Lawyers*, 87–90.

26. Rhode, *Trouble with Lawyers*, 87–120. See also Steven Gillers, "The Legal Industry of Tomorrow Arrived Yesterday: How Lawyers Must Respond," in *The Relevant Lawyer: Reimagining the Future of the Legal Profession* (Chicago, Ill.: ABA Standing Committee on Professionalism, Center for Professional Responsibility, 2015), 13–23; Thomas D. Morgan, "The Shift to Institutional Law Practice," in *The Relevant Lawyer: Reimagining the Future of the Legal Profession* (Chicago, Ill.: ABA Standing Committee on Professionalism, Center for Professional Responsibility, 2015), 143–155; and Krantz, *Legal Profession*, 83–87.

27. Rhode, *Trouble with Lawyers*, 90–98. Susskind observes that through the Legal Services Act 2007, England and Wales sanctioned the creation of "alternative business structures," or entities that permit (1) nonlawyers to run legal establishments, (2) outside investors to fund legal businesses, and (3) nonlawyers to be partners in law firms. Richard Susskind, *Tomorrow's Lawyers: An Introduction to Your Future* (New York, N.Y.: Oxford University Press, 2013), 6–7.

28. Morgan, "Shift to Institutional Law Practice," 153–154; Rhode, *Trouble with Lawyers*, 98–99.

29. Rhode, *Trouble with Lawyers*, 117. See also ibid., 99–102, 116–120. In England, the Legal Services Act 2007 sanctions ABS, thus authorizing outside investment and ownership in law firms. In Australia, in 2001 and afterward, many states legally allow "incorpo-rated legal practices" that permit similar outside investment and ownership. Laurel S. Terry, "Globalization and Regulation," in *The Relevant Lawyer: Reimagining the Future of the Legal Profession* (Chicago, Ill.: ABA Standing Committee on Professionalism, Center

for Professional Responsibility, 2015), 161–162. Studies examining how they operate are found in Mark S. Smith, "A Sea Change in England," in *The Relevant Lawyer: Reimagining the Future of the Legal Profession* (Chicago, Ill.: ABA Standing Committee on Professionalism, Center for Professional Responsibility, 2015), 171–196; and Simon Chester, "Canada: The Road to Reform," in *The Relevant Lawyer: Reimagining the Future of the Legal Profession* (Chicago, Ill.: ABA Standing Committee on Professionalism, Center for Professional Responsibility, 2015), 197–217.

30. Rhode, *Trouble with Lawyers*, 102–106; Rhode, *In the Interests of Justice*, 156–157.

31. Rhode, *Trouble with Lawyers*, 106–107 (New York pilot program quote); Rhode, *In the Interests of Justice*, 157–158 (Bloody Mary quote).

32. American Bar Association, "National Lawyer Regulatory Data Bank," accessed June 13, 2016, from www.americanbar.org/groups/professional_responsibility/services/databank .html. See also Debra Moss Curtis, "Attorney Discipline Nationwide: A Comparative Analysis of Process and Statistics," *Journal of Legal Education* 35 (2011): 209–337.

33. Attorney Registration and Disciplinary Commission, "Annual Report: 2015," accessed June 13, 2016, from www.iardc.org/AnnualReport2015Highlights.pdf, 25.

34. Supreme Court of Ohio, "Disciplinary Process," accessed June 13, 2016, from www .supremecourt.ohio.gov/Boards/BOC/Flowchart_legal.pdf. To illustrate, California's process is similar to Ohio's, though the state bar's Office of Chief Trial Counsel works with the State Bar Court to investigate, review, and recommend action to the Supreme Court for final resolution. State Bar of California, "Attorney Discipline Report for Year Ending December 31, 2015," accessed June 13, 2016, from www.calbar.ca.gov/LinkClick .aspx?fileticket=1fA6XzPn3gE%3d&tabid=224&mid=1534. See also Florida's system at Florida Bar, "Discipline Roadmap," accessed June 13, 2016, from www.floridabar.org/tfb/ TFBConsum.nsf/0a92a6dc28e76ae58525700a005d0d53/38b9889aff47178e85257f94005b be75!OpenDocument.

35. In California (2015), of 15,796 grievance filings, 990 (6 percent) resulted in formal discipline. State Bar of California, "Attorney Discipline Report," iv. In Texas (2014–2015), of 28,875 total phone, mail, and email contacts to the Client–Attorney Assistance Program, 1,094 dispute resolutions were conducted, and 318 total sanctions (1 percent of total contacts) were issued. State Bar of Texas, "Annual Report 2014–2015," accessed June 13, 2016, from www.texasbar.com/Content/NavigationMenu/AboutUs/StateBarPresident/ ExecutiveTeam/SBOTAnnualReport.pdf. In Illinois (2015), of 5,561 investigations, 3 percent resulted in filings of formal charges, with a total of 126 sanctions issued by the Illinois Supreme Court. Attorney Registration and Disciplinary Commission, "Annual Report: 2015."

36. State Bar of California, "Attorney Discipline Report," v.

37. In New York's unified court system, disciplinary proceedings are handled by committees in conjunction with the court and the relevant jurisdiction where the misconduct allegedly took place. Unless formal action is taken in court, complaints and their investigation are sealed and deemed private and confidential. Appellate Division, Second Judicial Department, New York, "Attorney Matters," accessed June 13, 2016, from www.nycourts.gov/courts/ad2/attorneymatters_ComplaintAboutaLawyer.shtml#_ Disciplinary_Proceedings_are.

38. Rhode, *Trouble with Lawyers*, 107–115.

39. In response to Chief Justice Warren Burger's complaint that law schools did not adequately train students with practice and professionalism skills, the Clare Proposal, implemented through Indiana and South Carolina's judiciaries, conditioned law licensure upon the completion of specific courses that were tailored to fix the problems Burger identified. Valentine, "Flourish or Founder," 496–497; Task Force on Law Schools and the Profession, *Learning Education and Professional Development: An Educational Continuum* (Chicago, Ill.: American Bar Association Section of Legal Education and

Admissions to the Bar, 1992) (the "MacCrate Report"); William M. Sullivan et al., *Educating Lawyers: Preparation for the Profession of Law* (Stanford, Calif.: Carnegie Foundation for the Advancement of Teaching, 2007); and American Bar Association Task Force on the Future of Legal Education, *Report and Recommendations*.

40. Rhode, *In the Interests of Justice*, 186. There are also structural and practical (if not discriminatory) consequences of using case dialogue law training. Because most law schools have an established first-year curriculum, at semester's end the results of the final examinations (which are based on a curve) determine student rankings and whether the "elite" of the entering class will join the school's law review, a prestigious honor that opens many professional doors (judicial clerkships, prestigious law firm employment, and the like); but the rest of the class is relegated to an inferior status with limited paths of professional advancement. Sullivan et al. *Educating Lawyers*, 7. See also Valentine, "Flourish or Founder," 482–505.

41. See, e.g., American Bar Association Section of Legal Education and Admissions to the Bar, *Legal Education and Professional Development: An Educational Continuum (Report of the Task Force on Law Schools and the Profession: Narrowing the Gap)* (Chicago, Ill.: American Bar Association, 1992); Sullivan et al., *Educating Lawyers*; Roy Stuckey et al., *Best Practices for Legal Education: A Vision and a Roadmap* (Columbia, S.C.: Clinical Legal Education Association, 2007). See also Valentine, "Flourish or Founder," 475–476.

42. James E. Moliterno, *The American Legal Profession in Crisis: Resistance and Responses to Change* (New York, N.Y.: Oxford University Press, 2013), 232. See also Michael Cassidy, "Reforming the Law School Curriculum from the Top Down," *Journal of Legal Education* 64 (2015): 428–442; Mitu Gulati, Richard Sander, and Robert Sockloskie, "The Happy Charade: An Empirical Examination of the Third Year of Law School," *Journal of Legal Education* 51 (2001): 235–266; Lynn M. LoPucki, "Dawn of the Discipline-based Law Faculty," *Journal of Legal Education* 65 (2016): 506–542; Philip G. Schrag, "MOOCS and Legal Education: Valuable Innovation or Looming Disaster?," *Villanova Law Review* 59 (2014): 83–134; and Symposium, "How to Fix Law School: Six Experts Tell Us What They'd Change," *New Republic* (July 23, 2013), accessed October 25, 2015, from www .newrepublic.com/article/113983/how-fix-law-school-symposium.

43. American Bar Association Task Force on the Future of Legal Education, *Report and Recommendations*.

44. Harry T. Edwards, "Another 'Postscript' to 'the Growing Disjunction between Legal Education and the Legal Profession,'" *Washington Law Review* 69 (1994): 561–572; Ronald K. L. Collins, "On Legal Scholarship: Questions for Judge Harry T. Edwards," *Journal of Legal Education* 65 (2016): 637–660.

45. American Bar Association Task Force on the Future of Legal Education, *Report and Recommendations*, 7. See also Adam Liptak, "Keep the Briefs Brief, Literary Justices Advise," *New York Times* (May 20, 2011), accessed June 16, 2016, from www.nytimes .com/2011/05/21/us/politics/21court.html?_r=0 (Chief Justice Roberts's quote); Harry T. Edwards, "The Growing Disjunction between Legal Education and the Legal Profession," *Michigan Law Review* 91 (1992): 34, 38–39, 59–63; Edwards, "Another 'Postscript,'" 561–572; and Collins, "On Legal Scholarship," 637–645.

46. Collins, "On Legal Scholarship," 646–647; Edwards, "Another 'Postscript,'" 563. See also Valentine, "Flourish or Founder," 481, 486 (detailing law academy's hostility and resistance to change).

47. Robin L. West, *Teaching Law: Justice, Politics, and the Demands of Professionalism* (New York, N.Y.: Cambridge University Press, 2014), 209.

48. American Bar Association Task Force on the Future of Legal Education, *Report and Recommendations*, 16.

49. Susskind, *Tomorrow's Lawyers*, 4–5.

50. Jay Gary Finkelstein, "Practice in the Academy: Creating 'Practice-Aware' Law Graduates," *Journal of Legal Education* 64 (2015): 622, 627–628. Being "practice aware" means that law graduates must be taught practice skills, but also learn how to comprehend how legal doctrine relates to legal practice. Ibid., 630–631. See also Paula Littlewood and Stephen Crossland, "Alternative Legal Service Providers: Filling the Justice Gap," in *The Relevant Lawyer: Reimagining the Future of the Legal Profession*, ed. Paul A. Haskins (Chicago, Ill.: American Bar Association Center for Professional Responsibility, 2015); and Susskind, *Tomorrow's Lawyers*, 18–19.

51. Susskind, *Tomorrow's Lawyers*, 3–14. See, generally, Krantz, *Legal Profession*; and Rhode, *Trouble with Lawyers*.

52. Susskind, *Tomorrow's Lawyers*, 56–57, 79–80.

53. Ibid., 109–131. The quotation is from ibid., 136.

54. For an empirical examination of judicial decision making affecting the scope and nature of civil Gideon rights, see Christopher P. Banks, Lisa Hager, and Elsa Gonzalez, *Civil Legal Aid as a Basic Human Right*, a paper prepared for the 2015 Annual Meeting of the American Political Science Association (September 3–6, 2015, San Francisco, California) (on file with author).

55. American Bar Association Commission on the Future of Legal Services, *Report on the Future of Legal Services in the United States*, accessed September 24, 2016, from http://abafuturesreport.com/#1.

56. Robert Ambrogi, "ABA Future Panel Calls for Broad Changes in Legal Services," *Above the Law* (August 8, 2016), accessed September 24, 2016, from http://abovethelaw.com/2016/08/this-week-in-legal-tech-aba-future-panel-calls-for-broad-changes-in-legal-services/. See also American Bar Association Commission on the Future of Legal Services, *Report on the Future of Legal Services in the United States*, 17.

Index